CHÁVEZ: THE REVOLUTION WILL NOT BE TELEVISED

Nonfictions is dedicated to expanding and deepening
the range of contemporary documentary studies.
It aims to engage in the theoretical conversation
about documentaries, open new areas of scholarship,
and recover lost or marginalised histories.

General Editor, Professor Brian Winston

Other titles in the *Nonfictions* series

Direct Cinema: Observational Documentary and the Politics of the Sixties
by Dave Saunders

Projecting Migration: Transcultural Documentary Practice
edited by Alan Grossman and Àine O'Brien

The Image and the Witness: Trauma, Memory and Visual Culture
edited by Frances Guerin and Roger Hallas

Vision On: Film, Television and the Arts in Britain
by John Wyver

Building Bridges: The Cinema of Jean Rouch
edited by Joram ten Brink

Films of Fact: A History of Science in Documentary Films and Television
by Timothy Boon

Documentary Display: Re-Viewing Nonfiction Film and Video
by Keith Beattie

Forthcoming titles in the *Nonfictions* series

The Personal Camera: Subjective Cinema and the Essay Film
by Laura Rascaroli

Playing to the Camera: Musicians and Musical Performance in Documentary Cinema
by Thomas Cohen

Rod Stoneman

CHÁVEZ: THE REVOLUTION WILL NOT BE TELEVISED

A CASE STUDY OF POLITICS AND THE MEDIA

WALLFLOWER PRESS
LONDON & NEW YORK

First published in Great Britain in 2008 by
Wallflower Press
6 Market Place, London W1W 8AF
www.wallflowerpress.co.uk

A catalogue record for this book is available from the British Library.

ISBN 978-1-905674-74-9 (pbk)

Book design by Elsa Mathern

Printed in India by Imprint Digital Ltd.

This publication was grant-aided by the Publications Fund of
National University of Ireland, Galway

CONTENTS

ACKNOWLEDGEMENTS

This is the place to acknowledge the help of Sue Clarke, Adam, Otto and Finn. This enterprise is dedicated to them.

My thanks to Kim Bartley and Donnacha Ó Briain who were consistently generous with their time; all unsourced quotations are taken from recorded conversations with them in August 2004 and again in August 2005. Thanks also to Lucia Astier, Richard Gott and Greg Wilpert; to Des O'Rawe and Sean Ryder – 'il miglior fabbro' – who read it critically; to Jonathan Williams, who committed to such an uncertain endeavour at such an early stage; to Don Christopher who gave brave legal advice; and to Eileen O'Carroll, who put it in good order.

PREFACE

In statu nascendi
In the process of formation

I should be precise about my own partial role in the story outlined in these pages. Having worked at Channel 4 television from its inception in 1982, I went to Bord Scannán na hÉireann (the Irish Film Board) when it was reconstituted in 1993, and was appointed its Chief Executive Officer.[1] I worked at the Board from October 1993 to October 2003 and this account of the production of a single film arises from my experience as one of its financiers. The role of funder is detached from, but supportive of, the independent filmmakers' realisation of the project, and I hope that the same terms of relationship pertain in this analytical phase of the life of the film. It should also be said that the front credit of *The Revolution Will Not Be Televised* referring to me as Executive Producer was not contractually necessary and it was the filmmakers' own decision – made with generosity and without consultation.

One aspect of writing this account of the film that has been particularly surprising for me is why the exploration of such proximate events with those directly involved should encounter so many confusions and blurred recollections in people's memories, my own amongst them. If the succession of dates and events of relatively recent history are so difficult to pull into focus with precision and certitude, we should perhaps be more sceptical of any reconstruction of distant histories.

While drafting an early version of these lines in Hanoi, I was reminded that Vietnam is also a place where a previous version of socialism and nationalism sustained thirty-five years of virtually continuous war and eventually led to the defeat of the world's most powerful military industrial complex by a peasant militia. The extraordinary imbalances of power and prosperity between the points of the compass and the imperative of perspectives from the South of the world to mitigate the hegemony of the North cannot be overlooked at this time.

Rod Stoneman
Galway
November 2008

INTRODUCTION

Quis custodiet ipsos custodies?
Who will guard the guardians?

At around 10.00 p.m. on 11 April 2002 members of the military high command arrive in the Presidential Palace to demand the resignation of the government of Venezuela. They lead the country's President to an inner sanctum as government ministers circle around nervously in an atmosphere of terminal crisis. Dissident elements of the army threaten to bomb the palace unless the President resigns. The Economic Development Minister looks near tears: 'It is the victory of the forces of death.' Amongst those waiting in the corridor outside the closed room for news of the tense discussions are two documentary-makers from Ireland; they have been working for the last 18 months to realise a documentary portrait of the President and the fast-changing political situation in his country. Using small, portable digital video cameras, they film the ensuing calamity. This is one of the most dramatic moments in *The Revolution Will Not Be Televised*.

A documentary that had originally been conceived of as a 'personal profile and intimate portrait of Venezuela's President was changed utterly.[1] An electrifying drama unfolded as the film depicted a group of individuals, in potentially mortal danger, who were aware that they have been placed in the centre of historical events. Unexpected contingent factors had played a significant role in the filming of the *coup d'état* both on the streets of Caracas and also inside the Miraflores Presidential Palace where the film captured the most intimate images of a regime in its moment of peril. The interaction of larger-scale social and political forces with the detail of contingent, chance events and the responses of various politicians, soldiers and government operatives was suddenly brought into unique focus. *The Revolution Will Not Be Televised* was made by Irish filmmakers Kim Bartley and Donnacha Ó Briain, with Galway-based independent production company Power Pictures. It centres on the charismatic and controversial Venezuelan President, Hugo Chávez, and charts the seven months leading up to the dramatic coup attempt of 11–14 April 2002. The film provides an eyewitness account of the *coup d'état* and the extraordinary return to power of Chávez some 48 hours later.

The film had been financed by Bord Scannán na hÉireann (the Irish Film Board) with RTÉ (the Irish public service broadcaster); the British Broadcasting Corporation (BBC) joined in post-production. RTÉ screened a slightly shorter television version of the film, *Chávez: Inside the Coup*, in February 2003 in a series called *True Lives* and an immediate second transmission was arranged as a result of the strong and enthusiastic response from viewers. BBC4 showed it in April and BBC2 screened it within the *Storyville* strand on 16 October. Having paid for a licence to show the production, these television stations had the right to transmit immediately;[2] it was then sold widely and screened by television stations in Canada, Japan, Germany, France, Holland, Finland and Denmark.[2] *The Revolution Will Not Be Televised*, a feature-length version of the documentary, was distributed theatrically in the United States in October 2003. Opening in six cities, it grossed over $200,000 at the American box office – an exceptional performance for any contemporary documentary.

The Revolution Will Not Be Televised was immediately recognised as a well-realised, emotionally powerful and politically relevant film about Chávez, a new icon of the Left and a thorn in the side of the US administration. But it was the unique footage of an actual coup in process which attracted attention in film festival screenings and on television, and the documentary achieved a measure of global critical acclaim. The first screenings indicated to many, including the Venezuelan revolutionary government, that the film could play a catalytic role in the subsequent history of the country it sought to depict.

But controversy quickly built around the film and it was subject to an extensive critical and political attack in Venezuela, with over 10,000 people signing an Internet petition, culminating in several fiercely disparaging articles. 'The film amounts to propaganda for one side in a highly polarised political context' wrote Caracas-based journalist Phil Gunson in an article entitled 'Chávez: Inside the Con? Documentary and the Fabrication of "Truth"'. Gunson made sweeping denunciations of the film's 'obvious breaches of balance, fairness and accuracy' and offered an alternative view of Chávez: 'he is a fairly standard Latin American military demagogue, who openly disavows representative democracy (despite having used it to achieve power) and is now busily installing a dictatorship. By this account, his "wealth redistributionis neither more nor less than the cynical and clientilistic purchase of a military/civilian power base' (2004b: 30).

Under pressure the film was withdrawn from an Amnesty International film festival in Canada and the petition orchestrated by Wolfgang Schalk in the name of El Gusano de Luz (literally the Worm of Light), that had been sent to the broadcasters, resulted in an investigation by OFCOM (the Office of Communications) and the BBC Complaints Commission. Dossiers of detailed information produced to defend the film were 500 pages long and three inches thick.

In the article mentioned above, Phil Gunson also claimed that 'polls have consistently shown that a majority would vote for a change in government' (ibid.). The pressurised context of the contention around the film was the run-up to an important Recall Referendum that summer;[3] in the poll on 15 August 2004 Chávez won 58 per cent of the votes. He subsequently achieved 63 per cent of the vote in the presidential election of December 2006.

The remarkable trajectory of the film and the powerful reactions it provoked have engendered a range of unexpected and longer-term questions. The intensity of the responses caught even the filmmakers by surprise. People involved in film production often nurture ideas about the potential political effects of their films, but it is rare that the intervention of any one documentary subsequently plays such a direct and dramatic role in the politics of the situation it seeks to represent. It is not an exaggeration to say that the screening and discussion of this single film had a significant effect on that pivotal moment of Venezuelan politics.

In 1976 the German essayist and poet Hans Magnus Enzensberger wrote: 'With the development of the electronic media, the industry that shapes consciousness has become the pacemaker for the social and economic development of societies in the post-industrial age' (1976a: 20). Contemporary media, constituted by the digital formats that permeate the information epoch, have created an image system that is extraordinarily pervasive and powerful. From its title, *The Revolution Will Not Be Televised*,[4] the film indicates its dual focus on both the political events and the central role of the media in an exacting political process. In the context of the coup, the film examines the role of the Venezuelan media at the moment of dynamic confrontation. But both Venezuelan and international reporting fell well short of a clear or accurate picture of events.

With the exception of the state channel, Venezolana de Televisión, five of the six television stations in Venezuela were privately owned and they took strong and consistently critical stances in relation to the regime. From his election in 1998, Chávez made use of state television and radio for direct, colloquial addresses to the electorate each week. The documentary originally chose these as a starting point for its investigation and took *Aló Presidente!*, the name of the weekly transmissions, as a provisional title. Chávez established himself as a brilliant communicator, speaking for hours on television in an informal and folksy manner that captivated his admirers and irritated his opponents. But this simple programme format on a rather staid official channel is very different in response and effect from the flow of negative commentary offered on the more colourful, energetic and entertaining screens of the commercial channels.

While different and specific historical and national circumstances are always in play in contemporary political conflicts, the centrality of the media is now a constant. In the 2002 coup in Caracas, the partisan intervention of the media became increasingly important as the social conflict escalated into a plot to unseat the regime. Communication is a crucial terrain of contention in political conflict and it was the interaction of the media with popular power and the physical force of the state which determined the outcome of this moment of political jeopardy. Bartley and Ó Briain's film is the nexus of a number of critical issues in relation to both contemporary political filmmaking and understandings of the potential for radical politics to bring about change in the world.

PRODUCTION

Omnia mutantur, nos et mutamur in illis.
All things change and we change with them.

CONTEXT – VENEZUELAN HISTORY AND HUGO CHÁVEZ

In sketching recent Venezuelan history as background to *The Revolution Will Not Be Televised*, one must return to the nineteenth century, and Simón Bolívar. The daring, restless hero liberated the Andean provinces one by one from the Spanish Crown but realised too late that, once separated, the new nations of Venezuela, Colombia, Equador, Peru and Bolivia would never coalesce and that his dream of a 'grand union' would never be realised. Bolívar is the iconic hero and reference point for Chávez's Fifth Republic.[1]

Much of Venezuela's nineteenth- and early twentieth-century history was characterised by political instability, civil unrest and dictatorial rule. Following the death of Juan Vicente Gómez after 27 years in power in 1935, the long dominance of the military continued until General Marcos Pérez Jiménez, another uniformed tyrant, was overthrown in 1958. With the removal of Jiménez democratic pressures eventually forced the military to support the electoral process.

Since the demise of *caudillismo* (authoritarian oligarchical rule), Venezuela has enjoyed an unbroken tradition of democratic and civilian politics, though not without military influence. 'Venezuelans are so accustomed to make the army the arbiter of their political contests', wrote Rafael Caldera in the 1970s, 'that at any moment the most varied groups, for the most dissimilar ends, attempt to involve the army in new adventures to change our political reality' (quoted in Gott 2000: 81). A succession of seven presidents rotated between two parties: Acción Democrática (AD; a member of the International Socialist Alliance) and COPEI (allied with Christian Democrats). As Alma Guillermoprieto explained, in that epoch:

> ... political debate became a matter of pro forma electoral exchanges between two parties more interested in preserving the privileges of the ruling elite than in restructuring an increasingly unfair society. There was a great deal of corruption, a great deal of waste, and, as the rural population migrated toward the oil territories and Caracas, a huge accumulation of urban poverty and a dearth of public policy to deal with the needs of the poor. (2005a)

Despite widespread poverty, 90 per cent illiteracy, no health service and minimal transport infrastructure during this period there was some stability and gradual modernisation underwritten by oil exports.

Between 1974 and 1979, and again between 1989 and 1993, Venezuela was ruled by Carlos Andrés Pérez (Acción Democrática), who nationalised the state oil company, Petróleos de Venezuela (PDVSA). He denounced advocates of globalisation as 'genocide workers in the pay of economic totalitarianism' and lashed out at institutions such as the International Monetary Fund, claiming that it was the equivalent of a 'neutron bomb that killed people, but left buildings standing' (see Gott 2000: 56). He began a period of profligate spending, during which corruption was consolidated as a way of life. In 1989, in his second term of office, he was converted to the 'Washington Consensus' and arranged an IMF loan for $4.5 billion. When Pérez attempted to enforce a ruthless monetarist approach, economic conditions deteriorated quickly and the inhabitants of the Caracas shanty towns descended from their barrios to protest and begin a carnival of rioting and looting known as the *caracazo*. Dozens of people died as the President called out the troops and declared a state of siege. One Lieutenant Colonel Hugo Rafael Chávez Frías, who had been preparing his own rebellious intervention, was left feeling that he had missed 'the strategic minute', as he later confessed to Gabriel García Márquez (2000).

HUGO RAFAEL CHÁVEZ FRÍAS

In 1992 the same Lieutenant Colonel, by then the commander of a parachute regiment in Maracay, the capital of Aragua state, attempted a *coup d'état* and proposed to convoke a constituent assembly – a model borrowed from the French Revolution. The uprising quickly proved unsustainable. After the brief insurrection, he was captured but the regime gave him a chance to make a short speech in order to tell those who had rebelled to surrender and prevent a massacre. Chávez managed to accomplish in two minutes on television much more than the elaborately planned armed uprising. First he said, 'I take full responsibility', a statement people had not heard from any politician or public figure before. Secondly he said, 'Comrades: unfortunately, for the moment, the objectives that we had set ourselves have not been achieved in the capital.' Chávez's use of the two-word phrase 'Por ahora' ('for now'), placed in the public sphere, became an immediate catchphrase signifying a long-term aspiration that demonstrated his determination to return to the fray. The uprising of 1992 suggested that there could be an alternative political project for the country and, like the 1916 Easter Rising in Ireland, a failed adventure soon became a beacon around which support gathered, changing the longer-term aspirations of large sections of the population. Like Patrick Pearse and James Connolly, Chávez wagered on the 'triumph of failure'.

When released from prison in 1994, Chávez became a messianic figure; he toured the country arguing for a renewal of the project of a left-wing nationalism, that potent combination of socialism with the high-octane fuel of nationalism, that – some two decades earlier – defeated the Americans in Vietnam. He embarked on a determined strategic shift to democratic means to achieve power, which led to a decisive victory, with 56.2 per cent of the vote in the 1998 election.

He moved into Miraflores Palace with a promise to sweep away the ingrained corruption of several decades and outlined an alternative project for Venezuela – and for Latin America – that would break away from the programme of economic liberalism imported from the United States. As Richard Gott describes it: 'He sought to involve his neighbours in a fresh interpretation of the "Bolivarian" dream of the nineteenth century, the creation of an independent and original Latin America that would unite its forces against the outside world' (2000: 5).

MISSIONS

In a relatively short period of time, Chávez began a wide range of grassroots initiatives designed to produce sweeping social changes. Apart from increasing the minimum wage and significantly augmenting the wages of teachers and doctors, he also began micro-credit programmes and a Women's Bank. Early in 2001 he implemented a programme of redistributing land to the poorest farmers, handing out building materials and land titles to long-term squatters, and granting titles to the self-built homes of the *barrios*. The government has sent troops to neighbourhoods to repair roads, paint apartment buildings and assist in other infrastructural projects. Chávez passed a Fishing Law which gives artisan fishermen back the subsistence means that had been accumulated by larger, multinational companies and increased this activity as a resource with export potential. Mission Guaicaipuro aimed to protect indigenous peoples' livelihood, religion, land, culture and rights.

Chávez also launched a large number of missions through the active participation of the citizenry. Mission Robinson is a reading and basic numeracy scheme; in 2003 alone, one million people in Venezuela were taught to read and write. More than a million previously excluded students enrolled in school as part of Mission Ribas. Mission Sucre is a scholarship programme for university education and Mission Vuelvan Caras provides vocational training for work.

Mission Barrio Adentro, a scheme to provide medical care for slum-dwellers, has brought 20,000 Cuban doctors, dentists and auxiliary staff to the *barrios* offering free healthcare. Paid for by Venezuela's cut-price oil sales to Cuba, in Caracas and in towns and villages previously without permanent doctors or health services the Cubans have built their *modulos* (small octagonal brick structures with an office on the ground floor and a cramped flat on the first floor). There they have dispensed Cuban drugs and practised the preventative medicine that Venezuelan doctors, who had little presence in the *barrios*, refused to consider (see O'Shaughnessy 2005).

Chávez has been consolidating his strength amongst the poor – like any politician strengthening his electoral base – but has also been creating the widespread experience of grass-roots participation in social transformation, which will continue, whatever changes occur in government or national politics.

His social initiatives stretch beyond national boundaries. Chávez also took the lead in proposing a more integrated and unified foreign policy for Latin America and the developing world more generally. Provocatively, he offered heating oil and diesel fuel at below market prices to poor communities and schools in the United States. 'If you want to eliminate poverty, you have to empower the poor, not treat them as beggars', he said, and, echoing the ideas of his favourite American writer, Noam Chomsky, he warned that 'Americans must reorder their style of life, because this planet cannot sustain their irrational consumption, especially when it comes to oil' (in Gonzales 2005).

THE INDEPENDENT FILM SECTOR

In Ireland, as elsewhere, the last twenty years has seen the incremental development of an independent television and film production sector. This has been in response to new forms of funding – primarily from television stations entirely based on the publisher/broadcaster model, or traditionally integrated broadcast structures gradually subcontracting proportions of their output to independents. Alongside this, with different criteria and configurations, national film agencies evolved to support independent filmmaking in most European countries and in other English-speaking territories. For clear historical and ideological reasons the United States has never developed equivalent support mechanisms, leaving audio-visual production entirely to market forces. Significantly, individual American states and cities have tended to set up screen commissions, which concentrate on facilitating incoming production.

Over the last twenty years there has been a clear evolution of television funding which has seen the growth of bigger independent companies. The commissioning of television companies in Britain and Ireland quickly began to focus on a small number of companies in each area of programming which offered a larger infrastructure and a safer context for production. Of course this is a convenient, comfortable production base which eliminates much of the risk, unpredictability and danger of commissioning from small independents, but it also reduces the range of work; fewer dogs and disasters, but also fewer brilliant and extraordinary programmes. So finding funding for new projects for most small independents tends to be a protracted, precarious process; many individuals eke out a living in a diverse freelance economy, working in other fields or on other people's programmes in the meantime. In terms of documentary production, commercial ventures – such as distributors – tend to come into play when completed works are shown in film markets or festivals, and then are almost entirely centred on documentaries about sport, sex or music.

FILM PRODUCTION IN IRELAND

The provenance of the filmmaking team and this specific project should be seen in the context of the exponential growth of new Irish cinema in the 1990s. The recreation of a national film agency in Ireland in 1993 occurred at a time when the country was itself in a period of extremely rapid economic and social transformation. With incomparable speed, Ireland ingested the reverberations of economic flux, the complex and wide-ranging effects of a belated secularisation, changing gender relations and decisive shifts in the armed conflict in Northern Ireland.

A new situation presented itself in film and television, as Bord Scannán na hÉireann (BSÉ) was set up again in 1993 and I was appointed its Chief Executive Officer. The architecture of the new Film Board's policies could be sketched on something like a blank sheet of paper; it was an unparalleled opportunity for an advanced and dynamic cultural project. The Board's re-constitution after a long period of closure in the 1980s facilitated a new approach: it had been set up alongside a range of connected, concerted government policies such as a revived tax incentive and the encourage-ment of a recalcitrant national broadcaster, RTÉ, to spend a modest propor-tion of its budget on independent production. These new policies were carried through in short order by the then Minister for Arts, Culture and the Gaeltacht, Michael D. Higgins. Taken together, they had a transformative effect – an immediate and sustained growth in film production in Ireland with local and international impact.[2]

As a national film agency, BSÉ had developed an approach which encour-aged documentary-making on international subjects, while remaining atten-tive that each project was driven by an Irish team. The national film agency's remit was to build an indigenous documentary production sector which combined an emphasis on the telling of Irish stories with support for Irish filmmakers who wished to address the widest range of international subjects. The Film Board consistently took risks with new directors and encouraged them to transcend any residual insularity in relation to subjects and ideas.

GENESIS OF THE PROJECT

Donnacha Ó Briain had studied history and the Russian language at Trinity College, Dublin and graduated in 1992. He worked and travelled in the former USSR in the 1990s before starting out in television as a researcher. He began directing as a freelancer in 1997 on historical documentaries for TG4,[3] then moved to focus on more contemporary social and political issues. He had become involved in several human rights and social justice campaigns over the years.

Kim Bartley was raised in France by Irish parents and returned to Ireland to study languages at Trinity College. She began work in television as a researcher for RTÉ and first started filming during the Kosovo crisis in 1998. Following this experience she worked as Media Liaison Officer for the Irish charity Concern and went to Venezuela photographing and writing as part of the emergency response team in December 1999, at the time of the catastrophic rains and mudslides in the shanty towns outside Caracas. 'I found that people on the ground, the poorer people who were directly affected by the rains, had a lot of faith in Chávez. Everything was Chávez this and Chávez that. I'd read a lot about him after his election and it was fascinating to see the hype on the ground.' The first discussions and conception of the project began in the autumn of 2000. They both set off on an unfunded two-week speculative recce in Caracas at the end of that year. 'We had been put in contact with a distant cousin of someone who worked in the palace. We thought it would lead somewhere. He never contacted us, but the day before we left Venezuela we got a call from the intelligence section of the palace. We soaked up the atmosphere; there was a sense that something genuinely was happening.'

There is always a hidden financial pressure in carrying a project of this nature into production and Donnacha Ó Briain put it succinctly: 'I borrowed a grand to go so you have to push the project at that point.' On 29 January

2001 the partners wrote to BSÉ under the auspices of their newly-formed company Runaway Films, with an application for development finance.

This was followed by an urgent fax from Kim Bartley on 12 March: 'We feel that this is a crucial stage for the project, that the next few weeks could decide whether the film will get made or not. We would hope to travel to Caracas as soon as possible…' It met with an apparently bureaucratic response – I had scribbled a note on the bottom of their fax and given it to my assistant: '13/3 Lorraine,[4] can you draft a reply and phone him [sic]. In the application round – back to them in early April – pointless to meet now.' Apart from the erroneous and reprehensible assumption that Kim was a male forename, my note indicated a desire to avoid meeting the filmmakers while we were still deciding about the project; it had to go through due process in the application round. Although filmmakers often hurried to push their projects forward, we had learned to slow down their importunate advances, since we were unwilling to disrupt the assessment process, whatever the urgency from the project's point of view. The Board was a national film agency, and unlike a television news desk, it did not need to develop a quick reaction capacity. Given the constant and inevitable disputation that arises from funding decisions, we had to make a necessary effort to protect the fairness, consistency and the integrity of the specific selection process within BSÉ.

However, the outcome of our deliberations was positive and BSÉ provided initial development funding; on 6 April 2001 I wrote on behalf of the Board offering Runaway Films a £6,000 development loan.[5] As the term suggests the loans were, strictly speaking, repayable; but our approach acknowledged that they were precisely to support the high-risk research and development stage necessary for some documentaries and would often have to be written off if the documentary was never realised.

BACKGROUND RESEARCH

Any funders involved in the development or production process of an independent documentary are responsible for a number of projects at any one time. Financiers must inevitably place a large degree of trust in the filmmakers they commission. In this case, however, given my lack of detailed knowledge of Venezuelan politics or history, I undertook some speedy research and judicious sampling and reading. I consulted a few articles on Internet news sites and the independent journalistic website *Counterpunch*, and read 'The Revolutionary', an extensive article about Chávez by Jon Lee Anderson in *The New Yorker*,[6] to find other opinions which could be used as a 'second take' to construct a wider context in which I could place the filmmakers' views. A few short articles may seem a scant and inadequate level of investigation into a subject where one is investing significant public monies, but given the pressures on the time of those involved in television or other forms of commissioning, this is an unusual depth of research. This background reading was also crucial if we were to have an informed discussion on the shaping of the documentary at rough and fine cut viewings.

While accepting that the initial terms and the premise of their documentary on Chávez was broadly supportive of him, it was important to me that this starting point should not undermine the complexity and integrity of the final film. The construction of a film as an unequivocal hagiography undercuts its relationship with the audience, who will begin to perceive the piece as 'propaganda' and question its integrity. Kim Bartley describes the starting point: 'We had put in this notion of investigating Chávez – was he a demagogue? Was the media persona just that? What makes him tick? My sense had changed as we got closer; what we're seeing here is a guy who is motivated, driven, not the demagogue with another side, drinking, carousing. I began to see him as more transparent – what you see is what you get.' And in a flippant aside Donnacha Ó Briain suggested that 'maybe part of that was to suggest complexity to try to get the thing commissioned. You do whatever you have to do…'[7]

WORKING RELATIONSHIPS

My approach to working relations with independent filmmakers and my appreciation of the centrality of their role was developed in early Channel 4 television,[8] and was based on a clear understanding of the relative autonomy of the individual filmmaker, and a deference towards that. I had made films and programmes independently before becoming involved in financing other people's work and so I had some understanding of the funding relationship from both sides of the table. Insistence on full involvement and detailed editorial participation as a financier should be based on rational persuasion rather than on exertion of the implicit coercive power of the commissioning body on independent filmmakers. There is an implicit balance of power in the relationship: the funder or commissioner needs the film and the filmmaker needs the means to realise it.

In this case BSÉ, as the national film agency driving the project, had the lead role in the complex context of other funding bodies that gradually committed to co-produce the same film. There had been explorations in advance and RTÉ had indicated initial interest, but delayed a decision on funding. Each funder had different needs, priorities and dispositions, which led to different participation in the decisions which had to be made. Seen from afar, these influences might be construed as an intentional political institutional conspiracy. From the point of view of the anti-Chávistas, who eventually began to criticise and vociferously oppose the film, European television stations and agencies could be regarded suspiciously as one coherent, homogeneous, premeditated block. In fact, closer to the process, a lack of co-ordination or coherence between financiers can clearly be seen.

It is difficult to understand how a perception of conspiracy could be projected onto a process which has so many variables and in which it is rare to encounter co-ordinated views, let alone Machiavellian manipulations. Sometimes a documentary with multiple sources of funding – such as *The Revolution Will Not Be Televised* – can be subject to seemingly arbitrary decisions, or responses which have factors which are impossible to determine: individuals' taste or politics, the lack of space in a particular television schedule, the proximity to another project a broadcaster may already be involved in. However, to use a double negative, this cautionary note is *not* to say that television decision-making is *never* conspiratorial but in this, as in most cases, there was a significant diversity and little collaboration in the approaches of the various funders during the production. The only efforts at co-ordination between them took place much later, when the finished film was under attack. There are many examples of the complex mosaic of financing allowing skilful independent producers to move between the funders and maintain their autonomy throughout. The fragmentation of power and payment may deflect and soften the editorial influence of any one financier.

FROM DEVELOPMENT TO PRODUCTION

As part of a development stage financed by the Irish Film Board, we encouraged the filmmakers to shoot a short pilot film for this project. There are several advantages to making a pilot: the central protagonist becomes visible and it is possible to judge if they have enough on-screen presence to sustain a full-length film; it provides a taste of some concrete imagery and an indication of the film's potential flavour and feeling. It can also build confidence in the project and attract other co-financiers. But there are significant dangers of being judged on an underbudgeted, roughly-made, preliminary glimpse of fragments from a hypothetical project. Important commissioning decisions are often made on the first premature impressions of a pilot, which will generally be very different from the finished film. Because of this, it is always advisable to ensure that the pilot is viewed with the filmmakers present, who can then discuss the project with the potential funder and handle their response interactively.

Following the completion of the development phase and the production of a short pilot at the end of 2001, there was a minor hiatus because the application Runaway Films had made to the Irish Film Board for production finance on 31 May 2001 was initially refused.[9] They had applied to the Board requesting a financial contribution of €60,000 towards a total budget of €131,000. This represents a modest budget for a documentary of this scope being made over a long period of time. I wrote on 23 July 2001 turning down their Production Funding application. It was our feeling that in order to fulfil its potential, the team that had developed the project should, at this point, form an alliance with a company with more experience to produce the film and to raise the extra co-production finance necessary.[10] This logic was obviously accepted by Kim Bartley and Donnacha Ó Briain, who approached several small independent companies and eventually decided to work with a Galway-based company, Power Pictures. With David Power as producer, there was a speedy reapplication for Production Finance to the Board.[11] Perhaps it is an inevitable consequence of working with a more experienced producer and a slightly larger infrastructure as a whole (a producer and assistant were added to the original two-person team), that while the request to the Film Board remained at €60,000, the total cost projected for the film had risen to €200,000.

At this stage David Power tried to bring other funding to the table. The filmmakers pitched the idea at the market attached to the Stranger Than Fiction documentary festival in Dublin that September. The BBC, S4C and Channel 4 turned it down, but David Power mentions that Kevin Dawson, Commissioning Editor of Factual Programmes for RTÉ, 'expressed an interest in committing development support to the project and subsequently said that RTÉ could come up with £2,000 in development funding for Aló Presidente!'[12] In fact this did not materialise, although RTÉ made an offer of a presale of €10,000.[13] This was subsequently increased to €20,000. The idea for the film was also taken to a documentary market in Barcelona that October and pitched to a panel of European television stations. It may have been Kim Bartley's impression that the broadcaster's commitment came through slowly, but David Power, the producer, asserts that RTÉ made a firm offer at a date much earlier that the end of filming. The idea for the film was also taken to a documentary market in Barcelona that October and pitched to a panel of European television stations. Cees Van Ede, a commissioning editor from NPS in Holland made a €10,000 presale commitment at that point.

David Power also went to a documentary market in Amsterdam in November, 2001:

> I went primarily to meet with Nick Fraser to see if the BBC were interested. His department had been sent the proposal some weeks previously, but I was unable to get any response from them. At Amsterdam Nick dismissed the project as one that the BBC had no interest in. Essentially, the subject matter was deemed not interesting enough for a BBC audience who feel that Latin America is too far away to be relevant to their lives. But Kevin Dawson had proposed the documentary at the EBU pitching session, which went down very well with ZDF (who subsequently came on board) expressing interest in the programme for the first time.[14]

There may be discomfort embarking on a project without secure funding for the complete budget but licence fee deals (securing the right to show the completed programme) which are agreed late in the day, help ensure a certain autonomy and preserve the project from interference.

The result of reapplication was more successful and at the end of 2001 BSÉ offered a production loan of €63,000 as a contribution towards the increased production budget.[15]

CRUCIAL BREAKTHROUGH – ACCESS

The pilot film was necessary to indicate the strength of the potential documentary and to demonstrate that they had achieved the necessary access and proximity to its subject. Independent journalist Michael McCaughan caught up with the project after the coup:

> It hadn't looked too good for them really. It was a long shot, this idea of a fly-on-the-wall documentary about any president in Latin America is obviously fraught because the notion of giving people access to what's really interesting about a presidency – behind the scenes, crisis, conflict – the elements which make a documentary really interesting, the idea of anyone in power handing that over is extremely unlikely. Their goal was out of proportion to their standing in Venezuela.[16]

The filmmakers had obtained a letter offering permission from the then Minister of Communications, Nicolas Rodriguez, at the end of their recce trip; and then they read in the newspaper on the plane home that he had resigned the day before and was now out of office. There was some apprehension that the agreed access might not hold, but this proved to be unfounded.

The reworked proposal indicated that they would continue making the film on the basis of the exclusive access to Chávez they had already obtained. It also made reference to realising a 'warts and all' portrait. Under the heading 'Chávez – The Man We Met' there is a section of the outline proposal giving a flavour of the texture of some of their encounters:

> As soon as we had arrived he offered us some of his supper – chicken soup and fried bananas. He then picked something up from behind a pile of books by Che and Mao – a packet of pasta. He turned to us, paused with a quizzical look, raised the packet aloft and asked: 'Have you tried this

stuff? No? It's top class, you really should, very tasty ... and look, look' and he ran around the table and held the packet up to our faces: 'Look here ... "Made in Venezuela"!' He then explained how he planned to revolutionize the Venezuelan economy, turning it from a country that imports most of its foodstuffs from the US, to a self-sufficient economy. Pointing to vast green spaces on the map he stated: 'We are going to re-populate these fertile territories ... give people land, money to develop ... The people are good, the people want to work, but they have been robbed for too long.' Then, mid-sentence, the phone rang and there ensued an animated lad's chat with President Pastrana of Colombia about a soccer match. All this confirmed our belief that Chávez will make for a fascinating and engaging subject.

The filmmakers' deployment of the detail of everyday life in proximity to public figures involved in momentous events was clever; this is always fascinating both for commissioning editors and eventual viewers.[17]

The application also contained a section indicating the filmmakers' political perspective and guarded approach.

More than anything we have been left with an overwhelming sense of the contradictions of Chávez and of his political process. His determination to bring about social change in Venezuela's weak and fragmented society requires the concentration of power which by its very nature risks a descent into authoritarianism and a departure from the progressive content of his revolutionary programme. We sense that Chávez is conscious of the isolation that this places on him and seems determined to remain in contact with the masses, to continue to not wear a bullet-proof jacket, to let history take its course. But is there a point where idealism crosses over to delusion and megalomania?[18]

This question provides an indication of the filmmakers' curiosity and open intelligence when embarking on a process of discovery.

When we met to discuss the project, the filmmakers outlined the evolution of their ideas for the documentary, explaining there was a 'change of idea – looking at the public persona in relation to the private portrait of the man behind the mask.'[19] In retrospect, Donnacha Ó Briain describes this stage of the project with the explication: 'We were always conscious of authoritarian trends within his style of leadership, his personal style, really shouting at incompetent civil servants.'

FILMING

The filmmakers left for Venezuela to start shooting their documentary at the end of 2001. Their return to filming involved building and confirming a closer working relationship with President Chávez and his entourage over the next couple of months if they were to film continuously and in proximity. Journalist and writer Richard Gott had contact in the palace with an adviser to the President, who was initially suspicious, and jokingly christened Kim Bartley 'the Irish spy'. Bartley explains the changing relationship:

> The notion of fly-on-the-wall filming was problematic for all his entourage. You came close with a camera and they would push you away. His secretary, a military man, could not understand why we had been given this access and did everything in his power to block us. We eventually managed to bypass him. Chávez called us in and overruled him.

Michael McCaughan puts it a different way:

> Kim read Chávez very well. She knew she needed 15 minutes with him to press the right buttons. After all the queuing and waiting, all the obfuscations and delays she got through and immediately got to the point; straight to O'Leary, Bolívar's right-hand man, friend of Daniel O'Connell in Ireland. Suddenly Chávez, a busy man, thinking about his next appointment, preoccupied with what's going on outside, was knocked offguard. Instead of massaging his ego she got to him with ideas.

This approach, planned by both filmmakers, involved giving him a book they had found in Green's bookshop in Dublin, a old edition of the memoirs of Daniel O'Connell's friend, about his experience fighting as a volunteer with the Irish Brigade in Venezuela alongside Bolívar in the 1820s.[20] Inside they inscribed the following text from Seán O'Casey from 1916: 'You cannot put a rope around the neck of an idea; you cannot put an idea up against the barrack-square wall and riddle it with bullets; you cannot confine it in the strongest prison cell your slaves could ever build.'

Their persistent presence filming day after day had an effect, gradually building trust and dissolving any self-consciousness as a result of their cameras. Michael McCaughan perceived the process from outside:

> Chávez was not always aware that they were filming. At some point they managed to become invisible. It was crucial to the success of the documentary they were there everyday, they got to know the President's men and women, who stopped seeing them as an intrusion, stopped seeing them at all.

As well as the filmmakers' informal style, the role of the lightweight DV (digital video) technology – its size, flexibility and ability to film in low light conditions – cannot be underestimated. The phrase 'caméra stylo' (camera pen[21]) was applied in a previous epoch to describe the school of anthropological French *cinéma vérité* that had emerged in advance of the *Nouvelle Vague* in the 1950s and 1960s; at this point the new technology has allowed the term to become even more accurate for digital filmmaking at the turn of the century (see Stoneman 2001).

IN THE EYE OF THE STORM – THE SEIZURE OF POWER

In this period, as their working relationships with Chávez and his inner circle settled into a pattern, in the outside world there was a build-up in the volume and aggression of the vociferous opposition to the regime and an increased anticipation of some kind of emergency or crisis. Donnacha Ó Briain recalled:

> We went with Chávez on a speedy road-trip tour of the country, it was interesting but so chaotic, *ad hoc*. We knew something was coming and he was out to rally the country and drum up support. He wanted to get people used to being on the streets. He had upped the ante with the land law.

In retrospect, Chávez confirms the premonition: 'We saw the *coup d'état* coming, but because of the disinformation and the lack of accurate detection apparatus, we were not able to discover when, how and where it was coming from. You could feel it in the air' (in Guevara 2005: 67). The beginning of a choreographed media spectacle was apparent on 7 February when the private television stations initiated a barrage of criticism, often clumsy and abusive. For the filmmakers this marked the beginning of an exciting phase. They could sense the heightened tensions in Venezuelan society as a whole and were aware of their proximity to the centres of power, to those trying to implement radical change.

On 11 April 2002 the dramatic events of an attempted *coup d'état* in Caracas emerged into international view. Large-scale street protests by the opposition had been countered by demonstrations of Chávez loyalists. An armed forces breakaway group had issued a statement calling on Chávez to resign.

The lack of general background coverage on events in Venezuela in the world media up to that point meant that outside the country there was a lack of context for any understanding of these occurrences. A short and dramatic narrative flash on the world's television screens – another Latin American coup. This lack of context allows reports to feed on the myth and image of a Latin American banana republic in turmoil.

There was also immediate publicity in the Irish papers: under the headline 'Filmmaker describes the overthrow and return of Chávez', freelance journalist Michael McCaughan relayed Kim Bartley's experience as a witness to events in Caracas:

'I arrived in the centre of town just as the shooting started,' says Kim. 'I filmed for a while then took cover in a doorway. Whoever was firing aimed directly at the crowd, which was pro-Chávez. We filmed two dead bodies, both of them beside the podium set up to rally Chávistas to defend the Presidential Palace. A woman working in the Vice President's office identified the bodies as a legal secretary and an archivist, both working inside the building. A ten-year-old girl was then taken away, fatally injured. More shots. We ran for cover like everyone else. We made it to the palace through back streets as the firing continued and as soon as we got in the gate another sniper started aiming at the crowd…' (2002: n. p.)

Interestingly, in this report Kim Bartley is also quoted as saying that three of the snipers were arrested. Apparently this was a rumour on the evening and night of 11 April.

> People [the army, presidential staff, journalists] told us that they had been arrested after having been grabbed and in some instances pummelled by a mob, but there was no chance to get to film them. After the coup when we enquired we were told that they had been held in the palace complex that night and when Chávez and ministers fled/left the palace the new coup leaders took over 'responsibility' for the prisoners. After that they seem to have disappeared – rumours were they had been killed or allowed to flee the country. Interpol put out a search for them with their details and photographs online – one was Colombian, another a US citizen. We haven't followed it up since.[22]

Carlos Polanco, a government educational adviser, was also present that afternoon:

> I saw two snipers being brought to the palace by presidential guards, I myself pleaded with enraged people to keep them safe as they would have to confess who had hired them. They were caught in a building in the north side of the Avenue and others in the Eden Hotel which overlooks both groups: us in the Avenida Urdaneta and the opposition in the Plaza O'Leary. Next day they would be freed by the fascists and the security cameras which would have filmed their entrance were vandalized.[23]

The filmmakers stayed in Venezuela until July filming other material including the sequence, later to be controversial in terms of its chronological placing in the film, with a group of upper-middle-class women listening to an emergency and self-defence lecture.

POST-PRODUCTION

When Kim Bartley and Donnacha Ó Briain returned to Dublin, they brought with them 300 DV tapes, more than 200 hours of footage for editing. The ratio of 200:1 (shot footage to the length of the final film) was exceptional; most documentaries would usually be made with a ratio of 10:1 or 15:1. For linguistic reasons an experienced Spanish-speaking editor was needed to work through the volume of material. Kim remembered seeing a documentary about baseball in Cuba,[24] so they traced and decided to work with its editor Ángel Hernández Zoido, who travelled to Dublin and began the long, slow process of reducing and ordering footage:

> So the first thing we tried to picture was the structure of the film. We spent time talking about something like a script. To me, there's no difference between fiction and documentary. While I'm editing a film I never forget that it is entertainment; I mean: we are not writing history books or deep treatises on politics; we are making 'only' films. Something that people are going to pay for to watch and thus make them think, laugh, or learn things they didn't know before. So you must never ever let them get bored. And that was my first target: 'Let's tell an interesting story and don't let the audience get bored.'
>
> But the big difference between fiction and documentary is that editing a documentary is somehow like riding a wild horse: the events that you have registered with your camera can rebel against you and it's easy to lose the control and get lost inside your own story. You have to deal with a huge amount of rushes and try to find out the soul inside these images. There are always hundreds of stories sleeping inside the material and you have to find them and wake them up. But you have to organise them in a way that they become entertainment.[25]

As they began the long process of wrestling with the material they had accumulated, the concept was being reshaped en route. In a sense they were looking at it for the first time, since there was 'no way or time to view material in the thick of making it'. They were always conscious of the dangers of a relatively *vérité* approach: 'During the shoot we worried that it might be awfully flat, filming Chávez and people responding to him. What are we going to do with that?'[26]

As Ángel Hernández Zoido described it from an editor's perspective:

Once we had decided a first structure I began the cutting itself. I always use the same method: I watch all the rushes of a scene with the directors and ask them: 'what do we want to tell in this particular scene?' There are two levels of perception when you watch a film: there is some information you need to follow the plot and there is also the emotion you can transmit through the images. How you deal with these two premises is, for me, the most difficult and challenging part of editing. Once we have talked about it I send directors home and I start the cutting alone. I need a lot of concentration to do my work so I don't want anybody looking over my shoulder while I'm cutting a scene for the first time. I watch the rushes many times before I cut a shot. I learn every shot and I make the first cut in my mind. Once I know what I want, I start cutting in a somehow chaotic way (if you don't know what I'm trying to do). I can begin at the end of the scene and then jump to the beginning, or put together a couple of shots that don't match at all and let them stay in the film for hours before I find the matching point. So if you are the director and see these operations I know you are going to say: 'What is this guy doing? This is never going to work.' And even if you don't say anything I know what you are thinking. That's why I send directors home during that creative period.

In this particular case Kim and Donnacha didn't go home; they met in a different room in the studio preparing the next sequence to be edited. So when I had the first cut of the sequence we watched it together and discussed whether the target was achieved. At the beginning there are usually some stylistic questions that don't quite match with the directors' first ideas, but once you determine the editing style it all goes on faster. For me it is very important to approach the material through the director's eyes and sometimes it takes some extra time for experiments, but once you get it, everything is easier.

Clearly the coup had given the film a new dramatic centre, although the makers were anxious that the whole piece should not be entirely focused on it. They had initially planned a wider approach with a greater degree of context and depth about the politics of Venezuela and were reluctant to lose that breadth. 'The transformation of the project was in the edit, the coup crystallised things on an emotional level but we resisted it becoming a documentary just about the coup. We always wanted some historical dimension.'[27]

Interestingly enough, an update about the project sent out by Power Pictures at that time, aimed at other potential funders but copied to the Film Board, did not give the coup full prominence.[28] Only one paragraph on four pages centres on the coup attempt and there is very little material on the role of the media. The evolution of the central foci of the film gradually came into view in the second half of the post-production process. A key approach to the structure of the sequences was the idea of counterpoint – the dramatic relationship between and within scenes:

> The next section of the film presents a reconstruction of the April coup. Using exclusive interviews we piece together the remarkable events of those three days ... This part of the story will be told with pace and verve of a thriller as the audience witnesses the unfolding of an almost inevitable reaction against Chávez's vision and reforms.[29]

The six-month edit had its own intensity and drama – the process of shaping a single documentary from so much material. As Kim Bartley explained: 'We edited by day, viewed by night, slept in the edit suite. It was almost overwhelming.'[30] With Brendan McCarthy, the Film Board's Head of Production and Development, I viewed most of a two-hour version of a rough cut on 17 October 2002 at the Film Board offices in Galway. Such a viewing, no matter how informal, introduces a delicate dynamic into the editing process. Implicitly, as one of the commissioners, I was judging and advising on the work but to wade in too forcefully would create only disturbance and resistance; it is necessary to create a constructive and supportive atmosphere for this most subtle human interaction. In a particular and peculiar twenty-year trajectory working for Channel 4 and the Irish Film Board, I have viewed probably over 1,000 rough cuts with filmmakers; a process which, by bringing a detached and less involved perspective to the material, helps calibrate its production of meaning. The most useful attribute the financier may bring to the rough cut and the production process is precisely distance from it. When it works constructively these editorial suggestions may be more symptomatic and precise, but it is really a premonition of the response of 'real' viewers – the audience. Filmmakers are inevitably apprehensive about this process and become concerned about the problematic dynamic of some funders' rough cut viewings. As Kim Bartley suggested: 'some people make ego-driven comments, just to have an input for their own sake, put their mark on it.'[31]

At this stage, the long rough cut already indicated a strengthened focus on the role of the Venezuelan media in the political atmosphere that preceded the coup and, crucially, during the actual coup attempt; this dimension was part of the original intention, but it became substantial only when all the material was laid out and the shape became visible. After the coup, Kim Bartley and Donnacha Ó Briain had recorded careful interviews with all the ministers, security guards and journalists who were there during the events. They talked to them after the event as 'witnesses'. Many of these were attached to the account corroborating the main story as eyewitnesses from all sides.

Although the presence of the witnesses strengthened the evidence of the film they diluted its originality. I argued that although other filmmakers may well make different versions in the longer term, the specific strength and uniqueness of this piece was as a first-person dramatic narrative through the filmmakers' direct role and presence throughout. Although they still, at this point, intended to avoid using any voice-over, I proposed a logic to eliminate the planned 'witness' interviews. The implications of this were talked through, together with the proposition that the story of making the film should come into view and the filmmakers themselves should become more central as protagonists and witnesses. Kim Bartley recalls: 'We were still battling not to use voice-over and we were trying to use the interviews to move the story along; we were reluctant to make it personal and didn't want to push ourselves forward as a presence in the film.'[32]

There was pressure on the production budget as it evolved at this stage of the process. Paddy McDonald, the Board's Business Officer, had to delay finalising the legal contract and restrict the cash flow until the whole budget was in place. This was always necessary to limit the Board's exposure in case a project collapsed before it was fully funded. We continued dripfeeding the post-production, but on a restricted basis. Following this viewing, however, my sense of and enthusiasm for the project enabled me to be more concrete about its potential when I made a phone call on 21 October to Nick Fraser, whom I had known previously as a colleague in Channel 4 television in the late 1980s. He was now working for the BBC commissioning long documentaries for a strand of programmes entitled *Storyville*. I rang him supporting the filmmakers as part of their effort to bring other allies into partnership on the co-production. My notes of the phone call indicate that he was still undecided, explaining that Roland Keating, the then-controller of BBC 2, had deferred the thought of a presale using the extraordinary and revealing phrase, 'we've done Chávez.'[33]

The BBC pre-purchase of a licence fee came through and they were sent a rough cut on 21 December. They focused on their misgivings about the voice-over, Nick Fraser apparently comparing it disparagingly to 'those early Channel 4 documentaries from the eighties'. The filmmakers themselves felt that the commentary was at an early stage, ropey and badly phrased; it was polished up but not significantly changed in terms of content. As Kim Bartley explained:

> They wanted the voice-over to be more opinionated, to get the boot in, to have a point of view – my feeling was they wanted it against Chávez although that was never made explicit. They wanted to have a historical pen picture of Chávez early on which would have broken the *vérité* flow and this was resisted. They asked for a 'dramatic' opening for the television version, which they got. After the RTÉ transmission all these issues had been resolved and all that remained were some bits of voice-over that they didn't like – we made a few minor concessions but stood firm on anything we felt strongly about. They also wanted a more personal voice-over: 'We were getting scared…' At a certain stage Nick Fraser suggested getting an older, more experienced director to come into the edit and assist – needless to say we reacted very strongly to this and it never happened.

Whatever the vagaries of discussions with broadcasters and financiers, there was enough time for the detailed discussion necessary to work them through to a satisfactory conclusion. Starting in mid-July 2002, they had intended to edit and complete the film in ten weeks, in fact it took until

February 2003 – seven months later. It is clear that the process of working and reworking material for such a protracted period is key to the film's eventual strengths. The implications of structuring decisions and the plasticity of individual sounds and images need working through in detail and across time. Most current affairs and factual television is produced quickly and there is no opportunity for a slower, more considered process. This is part of a deeper problem in Western countries where the media provide the spectacle of knowledge – part of an image system where 'all is shown, all is talked about, all the time' – but on a very limited analytical basis and from extremely constrained points of view.

RECEPTION

Mens agitat molem.
A mind sets the material mass in motion.

FINISHED VERSIONS

The film was completed in two versions: *Chávez: Inside the Coup*, a 52-minute programme to fit one hour television 'slots' and *The Revolution Will Not Be Televised*, a 74-minute feature-length version. In the longer version the film opens with Chávez being received with popular enthusiasm while touring country areas. Wearing his characteristic scarlet beret and bright national colours his speeches at rallies denounce the 'savage project of neo-liberalism' and implicitly anticipate the challenge to come: 'I've had to withstand huge international pressures, but I don't care if it means that one day I'll have to go to the gates of hell to defend the people of Venezuela.'

There is increasing pressure on him from local and international media. In voice-over the filmmakers explain that seven months before the coup they had started to make a film with the intention of getting behind the layers of myth and rumour that surrounded Chávez.[1] After explaining some of the historical context to his rise to power in Venezuela, the film shows Chávez's charismatic personal touch, responding to citizens during a phone-in on *Aló Presidente*, the informal weekly television programme. Going about his daily schedule, Chávez's individual informal contact with soldiers and advisers works to increase loyalty and support both inside and outside the Presidential Palace. Meanwhile extracts from private television stations indicate a relentless campaign against the President led by overt hostility from the country's North American neighbours.

The voice-over continues: 'As a young army officer he had led a coup in 1992 against the government of the day, he failed and went to prison, but it turned him into a popular hero.' In a quieter interview Chávez tells the revealing story of a childhood memory about his grandfather, an ancestor who had always been depicted as a murderer in his family. In 1890 he had killed a *coronel* who had made a young orphaned girl pregnant, gaining this reputation as a murderer, but had joined Bolívar and his revolutionary fighters.

In January 2002 Venezuela is polarised; there is energetic support for Chávez and his new constitution although on the prosperous side of town a residents' association meets and well-dressed ladies disparage Chávez and his supporters. Fearing the descent into communism and totalitarianism they are trained to use small arms in self-defence. 'It's important to keep an eye on domestic servants', suggests the instructor.

The issue of the disposition of the country's oil revenues looms large as Chávez attempts to control the oil industry, there is a backlash and – by February 2002 – a significant increase of tension. Director of Central Intelligence George Tenet expresses the Central Intelligence Agency's (CIA) concerns to the American Congress. A Venezuelan general issues a warning on television and proposes that Chávez step down.

On 11 April crowds build to a confrontation as an opposition march changes route and converges on the Presidential Palace. Without warning sniper fire hits some unarmed and peaceful marchers. Private television channels blame Chávez supporters for the deaths. A dramatic shot of 'the shooters on the bridge' is misconstrued to make it appear they are firing their handguns at the opposition march.

There is confusion in the palace, a government broadcast is interrupted and members of the military high command enter to demand Chávez's resignation. The President refuses to resign, but consents to accompany the officers just before the deadline of their threat to bomb the palace.

The next morning a television chat show reveals the careful planning involved in the *coup d'état*. Dignitaries, media pundits and coup leaders are present as Pedro Carmona is sworn in as the new President.

Meanwhile popular protest is building on the streets as Chávez supporters descend from the barrios to march on the palace. They retake the centre of the city as word spreads that Chávez had not actually resigned. People are killed in street fighting with armed police, a crowd converges on Miraflores Palace as the guard retakes the building. Chávez's ministers return from hiding and attempt to stabilise the situation. Channel 8, the state television signal, is re-established and, in absence of Chávez, the Vice President is constitutionally sworn in as acting President. The government regains full military control of the country as an army general announces on television that the army respects the constitution.

Chávez descends from the night sky in a helicopter, passing the filmmakers as he sweeps through the palace corridor – 'Show me the video of the night they took me away ... I knew we'd be back.' Chávez makes a speech calling for calm and reconciliation.

TRANSMISSIONS

RTÉ broadcast *Chávez: Inside the Coup*, the hour-long television version in Ireland, at 10.00 p.m. on 18 February 2003, as part of a series called *True Lives*. There was an extraordinary and unanticipated public reaction to the screening: lively debates on radio talk shows, newspaper articles and a deluge of emails to the producers followed. Irish viewers seized on the exhilarating image of the popular reaction to the attempted coup; the expression of 'people's power' in the face of an anti-democratic attempt to seize control of government inspired an enthusiastic response, despite people's unfamiliarity with the history and politics of Venezuela or Latin America more generally.

At the inception of the project the filmmakers had conceived of its potential audience as a niche market – those already interested in Latin America and anti-globalisation issues. The shock of the impact of the first transmission indicated 'how it captured the imagination of those who didn't even know where Venezuela was, but it was the power to the people thing that grabbed their imagination', as Kim Bartley described it. The programme was immediately recognised as a triumph of political television. There was such an immediate and positive response from viewers and critics that RTÉ took the most unusual step of arranging for a speedy repeat broadcast.

The success of the piece on television was immediately apparent and raised the question of whether or not the European television broadcasts were premature; should the film have been allowed to realise its undoubted international theatrical potential first? Over the years it has become increasingly difficult for documentaries to perform in a theatrical context, but there are rare exceptions with music films like *Woodstock* (Michael Wadleigh, 1970), and *Gimme Shelter* (Albert Maysles and David Maysles, 1970) about the Rolling Stones concert at Altamont, California. More recently a mystic, ecological film, *Koyaanisqatsi* (Godfrey Reggio, 1983), broke through and wildlife genres (often heavily anthropocentric) can perform commercially: *Microcosmos* (Cruz Delgado, 1978) and *March of the Penguins* (Luc Jacquet, 2005). More controversial political fare, such as Michael Moore's series of polemics – *Roger and Me* (1989), *Bowling for Columbine* (2002) and *Fahrenheit 9/11* (2004) – as well as Morgan Spurlock's *Super Size Me* (2004), have worked well at the box office. *The Yes Men* (2005) depicts some politically adept manipulation of the media and was made by some of the team who produced *Manufacturing Consent* about Noam Chomsky (Mark Achbar and Peter Wintonick, 1992)[2] and *The Corporation* in 2003.

With rare exceptions documentaries are restricted to the film festival circuit and television screenings, but the best sequencing is to use festivals to create an initial interest and profile, then exploit theatrical potential, and finally television. This mutually beneficial order is difficult to maintain when the film has currency or urgency, as in this case. The film festival circuit has grown enormously in recent years and, as festival programmers tend to look closely at one another's schedules, the reputation of a film like *The Revolution Will Not Be Televised* spreads rapidly, although curators' interest tends to fall off if the film has been previously transmitted on television.

Even if a documentary is made with television finance, transmission can be delayed or held-off to allow for a cinema release. This is to the mutual advantage of the filmmakers, distributors and television stations. I remember an experience with Michael Moore's *Roger and Me* when I worked at Channel 4. Alan Fountain, who was the head of the Independent Film and Video Department, had seen the partially completed film at the Independent Feature market and had committed a £40,000 presale to help finish it. I was working in the office when Colin Leventhal, Head of Legal Affairs, rang up to relate that he had Warner Bros. executives with him and they were asking us to hold off transmission for two years to allow them to exploit the film theatrically. I explained that we would normally be pleased to accommodate this but, unfortunately, that would not be possible because *Roger and Me* was already scheduled at the front of a season of American independent films in a month's time and that it would weaken, if not destroy, the planned season if we removed this documentary. I remember Colin's dry tone when he clarified painstakingly 'Rod, perhaps you don't understand when the word "ask" is a verb in a sentence with 'Warner Bros. Executives' as the subject, it has a different and more compulsory meaning...'.

Unfortunately the speedy television transmissions of *The Revolution Will Not Be Televised* in Europe precluded a theatrical run for the film. Ironically, the one country where this film had significant theatrical exposure was the US; despite initial interest from Home Box Office (HBO, an American subscription channel), there was no television company willing to transmit it.[3] The film also lacked a distributor to drive its theatrical release. Television inevitably exerts pressure for early transmission and the strong currency of the subject matter had meant that television commissioning editors were anxious to transmit sooner rather than later. In retrospect, the filmmakers inevitably wondered if the film could have achieved successful theatrical releases around the world, this would have helped build strong television audiences as well. Donnacha Ó Briain remarked that 'we needed someone who could see the international potential', and Kim Bartley said that 'there was considerable financial pressure to pay off debts – we needed a mentor or someone outside the process'.

FESTIVALS AND SCREENINGS

The film was circulated to international film festivals where it immediately began to win prizes. It won the Global Television Grand Prize at the Banff Festival in Alberta, Canada, on 11 June 2003, where it was judged best programme in the Information and Current Affairs Production and Global Television categories, beating 82 international productions in 14 categories, chosen from an entry of 900 films from 39 countries. The citation read: 'The best television programme in the world this year ... a wonderful story, brilliantly told.'

It won a George Foster Peabody Award and the Needle Award at the Seattle Film Festival. It also took Le Prix Georges de Beauregard International at the Marseille Film Festival and First Prize at the Three Continents Film Festival in South Africa.

There was some controversy around its winning Best International Documentary and Best Newcomer at the Grierson Documentary Awards, London, because London-based Venezuelan filmmakers wrote to the jury suggesting there were inaccuracies in its depiction of events. All this took place in the discursive context of enthusiastic reviews: 'A superior example of fearless filmmakers in exactly the right place at the right time ... sequences spark with a vibrant tension and uncertainty. It is true *cinéma vérité*' wrote Scott Foundas in the film and television trade magazine *Variety*. Mobilising unrestrained hyperbole, the *Sunday Independent* was of the view that it was 'undoubtedly one of the finest pieces of journalism within living memory'. 'A fascinating front-row seat for what could be history's shortest-lived coup', was the opinion of V. A. Musetto in *The New York Post*. 'It proves again that the best documentaries currently outshine Hollywood features as the most watchable, energising, and relevant movies around', wrote Jonathan Rosenbaum in *Chicago Reader*. [4] The website metacritic.com assembled 24 American critics and gave the film an average score of 82/100. [5]

The film was screened in Los Angeles as part of a short Irish Film Board season at the Egyptian Theatre (run by the American Cinemateque) on Hollywood Boulevard in March 2003. The warm public reception at this screening was noticed by staff at the venue; the head of its distribution operation, David Shultz, offered to release it theatrically in the United States. In deciding on an eventual release date for its theatrical distribution, Shultz's instinctive sense of marketing and timing took in the microclimate of internal politics in the US. He delayed the eventual release date for nine months after he had first agreed theatrical rights, until the first phase of fighting in the second Gulf War had subsided. As the insurgency against the occupation of Iraq began to build, so too did the peace movement in the United States, which created a better climate for the film's release.

The film was released theatrically in the US on 5 November 2003. Opening in six cities it grossed over $200,000 at the American box office – exceptional for a documentary of any kind – although this level of return does not yield a net profit. Individual screenings occasionally generated heated reactions. Marina Levitina was a Russian student studying Soviet cinema at Harvard University:

My husband and I went to see *The Revolution Will Not Be Televised* at the Kendall Theater in Cambridge, Massachusetts. The theatre was packed. When the film was almost over, but before the credits stopped rolling and the lights were turned on, a woman in her mid-forties stood up a few rows behind us and said, in a loud voice with a heavy Latin American accent: 'What you just saw is only part of the truth! The other side is not represented at all in this film!' Immediately a man in a row in front of her replied loudly that the film was indeed truthful, and it was people like her who were concealing the truth. Several people stood up and a loud argument erupted across the whole theatre. Soon, some people started to chant 'El Pueblo unido jamás será vencido!' The credits were still rolling. The woman and the man who started the argument were in such an emotional state that the argument was close to turning into a fistfight. At that point an usher came in and reprimanded the woman who began the argument, and said 'everyone is entitled to their opinion, but people are here to see a film, and you are stopping the rest of the audience watching the film in its entirety.' The lights started to come back on at this point. An American couple in their sixties was sitting close to where the usher was standing. The old man seemed bewildered, he stood up and asked the usher: 'But who should we believe?'[6]

RECEPTION IN VENEZUELA

Kim Bartley took the film to Venezuela in February to show it to those involved. She also arranged a screening with Chávez:

He said he'd love to see it so we sat in his office and after about twenty minutes he said 'let's have something to eat.' He ordered some food and kept watching and didn't say another word until it was over ... he seemed to be quite emotional watching the coup part. Then he said 'my god it's so strange to see all that for the first time, it brings back so many memories.

I had never seen what was going on outside the doors of my office, when the minister was crying.' He seemed moved and was quite reflective.

Michael McCaughan speculates that 'the immensity of this documentary had finally hit him. In the abstract it's just another documentary on Chávez, there have been many. You have to experience it to realise that it could be a catalyst for something, it could change history. This is what hit him by the end of it and then he's on the phone to Castro' ('about something else!' interpolates Kim Bartley) 'and then it becomes "this is it"'.

Thus BSÉ agreed to waive its rights to financial returns from a sale to television in this specific territory and the film was shown in Caracas's biggest auditorium at the same time as it was transmitted on the state-owned and government-controlled Venezolana de Televisión, on the anniversary of the coup, at 9.00 p.m. on 13 April 2003. Hugo Chávez made a speech before the screening: 'Watch this film and you will see the face of the coup.'

There had been some anticipation of the film amongst pro-Chávez circles in Venezuela; according to Donnacha Ó Briain: 'We had privileged access to what was going on inside the palace and we knew that must have an effect on people. They knew we could see the humanity of previously demonised ministers.' This was enhanced as the film was emerging in a period of greatly increased tension; the opposition was entirely focused on the referendum/recall campaign. Thus the contending accounts of the coup were part of the argument concerning the legitimacy of the regime and the recent challenge to it, all of which fed directly into the fierce electoral contest. There followed a gradual build up of criticism as the transmission brought the film to the attention of those opposed to the Chávez regime. The storm clouds began to gather after the transmission of the film by Venezolana de Televisión.

The way in which we manufacture the discourse of what happened in the past impinges on the construction of the future. Histories, as Walter Benjamin (1973) suggested, are discourses of legitimation inextricably connected to the present and to the future. A myth had built around the events of the previous April. Donnacha Ó Briain recalled: 'One crazy version had it that Chávez had resigned – they had assumed that "after all everybody knew he is bad and a coward" – and there had been a vacuum of power. All accounts stressed the "vacuum of power". People had supposedly stepped in, acting responsibly for the good of Venezuela, then the poor started looting….'. The political conflict about the present found a focus in the specifically contrasting versions of what had happened in the recent past. Benjamin also wrote: 'To articulate the past historically does not mean to recognise it "the way it really was". It means to seize hold of a memory as it flashes up at a moment of danger' (1973: 257). A representation of one moment of history is deployed into the next ever-changing phase of current events. George Orwell invented the Party slogan in his novel *1984* (1949): 'Who controls the past, controls the future: who controls the present controls the past.'

Michael McCaughan showed the film to an invited group of anti-Chávistas of different ages and income levels in July of that year:

> There were some signs of fiercely anti-Chávez viewers changing their minds as a result of viewing the film – 'They lied to us, they never told us what really happened during the coup' … The hostile audience grew impatient at the images of Chávez blessing community projects and hugging the people, and they dismissed all signs of popular support captured on-screen. At least half the documentary was inaudible as a result of the running commentary of the hostile viewers. By the end of the programme, the general consensus was that the documentary was 'excellent' and reasonably objective, but that Chávez remained a dictator leading the country to a totalitarian grave. …Mineya Theisa, a lower-middle-class woman who watches only the anti-Chávez TV channels, said 'I think Chávez organised the coup himself', irritated by the irrefutable images she had been viewing. (2003: 6)

Having written a letter of complaint to RTÉ in July 2003, a Venezuelan television engineer and producer, Wolfgang Schalk, representing an organisation called El Gusano del Luz, affiliated with La Co-ordinadora Democrática, an opposition umbrella group, began a larger-scale, concerted campaign against the film two weeks after the BBC2 transmission in October.[7] This delay enabled those opposed to the programme to orchestrate their operation internationally, build the campaign effectively and eventually impede the possibility of American television buying the film.

In November the film was withdrawn from an Amnesty International Film Festival in Vancouver, British Columbia; John Tackaberry of Amnesty explained that their Caracas offices had been threatened and the film would, if shown, 'present some degree of threat to their employees' physical safety' (see Campbell 2003). In order to protect their employees, they felt they had to withdraw the film.

CONTROVERSY

The first enthusiastic encounters that audiences had with the film via television and festival screenings can be seen as a brief honeymoon period in retrospect; a lull before the film entered a fiercer arena of political attention and, to use a military expression, began to take a great deal of incoming fire.

When it came, the political and critical assault on the film was remarkable for the level of energy, attention to detail and ferocity of denunciation put into the attacks. The force of the critical onslaught can be understood as reflecting the heightened degree of political division and conflict in Venezuela. The filmmakers posed the rhetorical question of whether an autonomous civil society could deploy adequate resources to fuel such a concerted campaign against their film. Donnacha Ó Briain told me: 'They had several people working full-time on it for six months.'

Normally there are good reasons for not immediately falling in with conspiratorial accounts of a complex reality, but recent revelations obtained through US Freedom of Information documentation indicate that Washington has indeed been providing the Venezuelan opposition with at least $5.8 million a year through three organisations (see O'Shaughnessy 2005a). It has to be said that, even if there was financial support from politically interested parties, this does not invalidate the critique of the programme.

Following two programmes on Venevisión (a Venezuelan private television station owned by Gustavo Cisneros) with panel discussions dissecting and denouncing *The Revolution Will Not Be Televised* and a flurry of articles in the press, it became clear that the anger many opponents felt towards the film was connected with its high international profile. 'The fact that it had such standing abroad was a factor in the reaction at home', said journalist

Michael McCaughan. 'The Venezuelan middle and upper class are incredibly prejudiced, even racist. Everything recognised outside the country is legitimised in Venezuela. They are hyper-aware of how others see them and they see themselves through that prism. They care about what the respected elites around the world think about them, be that intellectual, political or whatever'.[8]

The idea that the film allegedly portrayed a false and distorted version of specific recent events in Venezuela, and of the Chávez regime more generally, to an international audience was bad enough; that the film should be blessed with the imprimatur of the BBC, with its connotations of fair and authoritative reporting, was intolerable.[9] Much of the outrage was exacerbated by irritation that the film could be associated with the BBC at all. Those who stood against Chávez (a group well used to more consonant and benevolent doxa[10] of received media opinions locally), found themselves confronted with a very suspicious film made worse by its presentation in association with a three-letter acronym signifying a distant and distinguished institution which bestowed the imprimatur of trust and truth.

As its dissemination by film festivals and transmissions on television continued, controversy and contention began to build around it, with a high level of complaints and responses reaching organisers, distributors and curators, culminating in the publication of articles, a petition and formal complaints in the autumn of 2003. From the point of view of those who opposed Chávez, *The Revolution Will Not Be Televised* 'constitutes the main weapon of the Venezuelan government to disseminate internationally a biased, manipulated and lying version of what happens here'.[11]

PETITIONERS

It was the transmission by the state-owned Venezolana de Televisión of the film in April that led to a manifestation of that relatively recent phenomena, an Internet petition. The petition followed Wolfgang Schalk's initial complaints, and also emanated from El Gusano de Luz. It quickly accumulated over 11,000 signatures. They were concerned that '*The Revolution Will Not Be Televised* is being presented as an author's film, as an objective journalistic research film, while it is really a very good plotted and accomplished propaganda operation, supported logistically by the Venezuelan government, with the aim of misleading unprepared spectators of countries who do not know the totality of events'.[12]

Some of the petition's 120 groups of signatures have been sampled on an arbitrary basis and selected examples are reproduced here.[13] The argument of the petition itself and its 18 specific points is discussed in the next chapter. Samples from the petition include the short comments that many of the petitioners have attached alongside their electronically 'signed' names. Nearly all reflect the discourse of the petition's argument and share the perception that *The Revolution Will Not Be Televised* is an intentionally propagandistic[14] piece of filmmaking that has been perpetrated by Bartley and Ó Briain with the naive support of '5 European TV Corporations'.[15] It is through the diversity of their short critical comments that one can discern the individuality and authenticity of the signatories. The global reach and electronic mode of the Internet also brings a wide range of international input, although approximately 85 per cent of the signatories nominate their country of origin as Venezuela. The form taken by this particular protest inevitably raises questions about the social groups and classes that have access to the Internet. The CIA website records that in 2002 there were 1,274,400 Internet users, out of a total population of 26 million, in Venezuela.[16] Clearly some social groups will pursue political expression through street protest, while others may use cyberspace.

An expatriate perspective from the United States is evident in the tone of Rosa Uzcategi (11508, USA): 'Vivo in Norte America, me vive huyendo de lo que presentia iba a convertirse mi pais … otra Cuba' ('I live in North America to escape those who want to convert my country … to another Cuba') and Claudio Guadagno (11530, USA): 'Chávez is nothing more than a bad communist and a killer'. Eduardo Ruiz de Sabando Ayestaran (11544, Spain): 'I have emigrated to Spain because is [sic] impossible to live in Venezuela with Mr Hugo Chávez the most corrupt and xenofobo [sic] of all government around the world.' Viewing the home country from abroad often engenders conservative and sometimes obsolescent attitudes, even when there is no social conflict at stake. As with the French and British communities abroad, or the Irish diaspora, there is a tendency for expatriates to espouse the preservation of an older and often anachronistic version of what the homeland should be. The calcified attitudes of the Cuban exile community in Miami have impeded the development of new relations between the US and that island.

The furious social turbulence on the home front in Venezuela drew an angry and defensive contestation from the country's expatriate community. The comments take many different stances within a defined range of positions, from the emotional directness of Lucila Ortega Carlos (16, Venezuela): 'SHAME ON YOU FOR FINANCING SO MANY LIES!!!', to the desperation reflected in the succinct distress of Carmen Cruz (6162, Venezuela): 'Help us!!!', to the considered tenor of Dr Antonio Sanchez Garcia (41, Venezuela): 'Please, a little respect for the democratic opposition.' Rosalba Guerra (22, USA) writes: 'Our Venezuelan president is a magician manipulating the media. Please trust the Venezuelan people. The mayoriaty [sic] wants him out of power and in Jail.'

More significant details of the experience of the events of April 2002 are inscribed by Blanca Travieso's simple statement, 'I was there', or Thais Bermudez (11589, USA): 'I went to Miraflores with my family by foot. We only carried flags. The government shoot against us. We have never forgotten that. Chávez is a killer and dictator.'

There are occasional notable dissident pro-Chávez views in the petition. Carlos Dorta (11525, Venezuela): 'The film "The Revolution Will Not Be Televised" is true, I was in the Miraflores those day the private tv stations prepared everything to destroy the best government that Venezuela had had, Live Chávez for ever, those person don't want to see reality [sic].'

But Maria L. de Muci (48, Venezuela) projects her suspicions: 'Those who financed this lie should be ashamed. It is very easy and romantic to have communist ideas from the comfort of a pub in London, or a café in the Champs Elysées, come to this latitudes [sic] and see with your eyes the reality.' The projection of imaginary affluent northerners cynically adopting left-wing postures at leisure from the comfort of their cafés and bars, like tourists of the revolution from afar, is revealing. Adolfo Blanco (89, Venezuela) writes: 'Quisiera saber la magnitud del pago que recibieron las televisionas europeas para convertise en cómplices del regimen criminal de Hugo Chávez' ('I would like to know how much the European televisions were paid to comply with the criminal regime of Hugo Chávez'). Or Manuel Aristimundo (56, USA): 'Given Chávez's absurdity to finance and sponsor Fidel's revolution, I wouldn't be surprised if these film shooters didn't get paid very good money to produce that kind of journalistic trash [sic].'

There seems to be a weird logic at work in imputing a venal motive for other people's politically offensive acts. Suspicion of distant institutions leads to a strange account of their rationale – they must have been deliberately and malevolently motivated, therefore it must have been a bribe. The ideology of the dominant social formation works to account for – and therefore to dismiss – opposition to its view of the world. As Colin McArthur wrote: 'A specific ideological project cannot tolerate contradictions. Hence the contradictions endemic in any complex situation must be defused, rendered manageable, ideally repressed' (1982: 124). The presumption that 'the filmmakers must have been well paid' is a way of understanding, of undermining and ultimately dismissing those who persist in dissent. Playing an American colonel who anticipates a Vietcong attack that night on his military base in the jungle, John Wayne stands proud in *The Green Berets* (John Wayne and Ray Kellogg, USA, 1968), and explains 'when Charlie's building caskets – when he knows he's got a nice box to be buried in – he is as brave as hell.' Clearly it helps imperial forces to understand how it is that the natives can continue to impale themselves on their bayonets.

There is a remarkable psychological intensity deployed in many of the comments; this dimension is interesting in its own right, and is often excluded from political and historical discourses. Richard Gott identifies some of the emotional fury as an intrinsic racism: 'Latin America is a white settler continent and there is always a fear of the aboriginal Other. Europeans are used to talking in class terms, but over and above the rich being terrified of the poor there is also the powerful fear of blacks and Indians developed over five centuries. Liberal Europeans do not expect racism at this level – it has been forbidden in Europe after 1945 with the shocking revelation of the Nazi holocaust.'[17]

These underlying psychological apprehensions may account for some of the emotional ferocity in much of the political expression; only a racist rage based on a fear of the underclass can adequately explain the degree of hatred aroused.[18] Psychological insecurities are central to the most formidable problem Chávez faces – the formation of an intransigent wider middle-class opposition, based more on ideology and racial antipathy than on the experience or threat of material loss. They are most alarmed by the way he has enfranchised the country's vast underclass, interrupting the cosy, US-influenced lifestyle of the white middle class with 'visions of a frightening world that lives beyond their apartheid-gated communities' (Gott 2005a: n. p.).

Venezuela-based journalist Phil Gunson has been persistently critical of most aspects of the Chávez project as correspondent for the *Economist* magazine; he became one of the film's fiercest antagonists writing critically in both the *Columbia Journalism Review* (2004a) and *Vertigo* (2004b).[19] Acknowledging a professional interest in the issue, he explained that he had pitched a proposal to write a freelance article to the foreign editor of a European newspaper, but it was apparently turned down because the editor had just seen *The Revolution Will Not Be Televised* and accepted the film's version of events. But he takes a snide and pejorative tone when describing Kim Bartley and Donnacha Ó Briain as 'two novice documentarists' (2004b: 30).[20]

Phil Gunson's *Columbia Journalism Review* article was taken up by other newspapers. The *Sunday Times* carried an article by John Burns entitled 'Irish film on coup "twisted the facts"', which quoted Gunson alleging that the filmmakers were guilty of 'omitting key facts, inventing others, twisting the sequence of events to support their case and replacing inconvenient images with others dredged from the archives' (2003: 7). Wolfgang Schalk is also quoted, characterising the film as 'a docu-fantasy' (ibid.).

EUROPEAN TELEVISIONS' INSTITUTIONAL RESPONSE

Predictably, the combination of a detailed critique, a large-scale Internet petition, individual critical articles and the sound of a distant furore was disconcerting enough to have its effect on the European broadcasters who had supported and transmitted the film earlier that year.

BBC commissioning editor Nick Fraser wrote to producer David Power on 12 December 2003 and copied his note to the other funders:

> I cannot feel as hopeful of avoiding further trouble as you do. The error on the end card is news to me. The footage used out of chronology (i.e. the

wrong demos) is a real problem – particularly, as you remark, since it has been used in a film dedicated to exposing the frauds of Venezuelan TV. It's not really defensible by any criteria of journalism.

We will not consider showing the film again until the BBC Programme Complaints Unit has finished its investigations. And it will be for them to judge – not myself, alas – whether these errors do or don't 'challenge the overall narrative accuracy' of the film…

My own frustration comes from the non-essential nature of these mistakes. If we were faced with anything really big – a forgery – I would be less upset, or more philosophical. But the footage could have been removed without any damage to the impact of the film. As you say, it doesn't affect the film's principle revelation – which is how a coup in Latin America is organised and implemented.

Kevin Dawson, the Commissioning Editor of Factual Programmes for RTÉ, wrote later that same day to the other broadcasters and funders, suggesting that he had drafted a rebuttal of some of the points made in the petition. These responses from inside fortress television have a double function. Firstly they are self-protective measures by commissioning editors anxious to distance themselves from a problematic programme; secondly they represent an institutional response rejecting external critique while creating a degree of internal room to manoeuvre. It is not surprising the television executives who had committed to the transmitted programme manifested institutional solidarity with each other but they supported the commissioned independents when attacked from the outside as long as the programme was defensible. Richard Gott argues that the television stations overreacted to the critique and petition: 'There ought to be more highlighting of the pusillanimity of the high-ups who get alarmed by the volume of protest. Maybe 10,000 email signatures seems a lot, but they don't seem to have done much investigation about the political input that this represented. This is probably the weakest point of the whole editorial/commissioning process, when there is a failure of responsibility.'[21]

Kevin Dawson was concerned about the textual 'end card', indicating the whereabouts of the coup leader, Pedro Carmona, subsequent to the coup.

The critics of the programme maintain that the on-screen text indicating that Carmona had 'fled' or 'taken refuge' in a third county was inaccurate and misleading. There may be some substance in this point.

Funding broadcasters should be made completely aware at approval stage of the status of material images used in an eyewitness documentary of this sort. As the subtext of the documentary was the relationship between truth and political power, centring on the use of television pictures, it should have been fundamental that there would be no dropped stitches, so to speak, in the fabric of the documentary.

I strongly believe – as does Nick – that a collective position will be most helpful. And I also believe that we should reach and hold a strong position so that the attacks of the critics, which are bitter and determined but for the most part scoring only minor 'hits' on the programme, should not be allowed to unfairly denigrate the very considerable achievements for which the programme has justly been recognised.

I had left Irish Film Board in October that year and the subsequent furore around this film clearly alarmed Mark Woods, the new Chief Executive Officer. His concern was with the financial implications: 'We need to figure out our position on how to handle any additional costs associated with further editing. Will BSÉ/IFB be expected to kick the tin? Will any expenses incurred by the broadcasters be expected to come first out? Also if the broadcasters do put out some kind of statement on this, then we need to have a spin position worked out amongst ourselves….'[22]

CRITIQUE

Caelum, non animum, mutant.
They change their sky (or horizon), not their mind.

ENTERING THE HALL OF MIRRORS

The first signs of a concerted response to the film's dissemination grew into a detailed critique published as part of the Internet petition on 21 October 2003. The main contentions were strengthened by their attachment to the mass petition, and they were taken up by the BBC and OFCOM (the Office of Communications) and had significant effects elsewhere; the controversy influenced and finally disrupted the sale to HBO. The following discussion takes a selection of the most substantial categories of criticism.

1. Allegations of specific distortion and misrepresentation

1.1 Pro-Chávez demonstration on 11 April – breaches of chronology
The petition states that the filmmakers used footage shot at another time and in another place during actuality sequences in order to mislead and give a distorted view of events. The term 'archive footage' is sometimes used to describe pre-existing footage integrated into the bulk of the material that was shot by the filmmakers themselves.

When showing the presence of presumed working classes in front of the Presidential Palace 'Miraflores' on the morning of April 11, 2002, the film used images of a concentration that happened on a different day and in a different city in Venezuela, where people appear happily singing, with children, while that day members of the government were really convoking people aggressively to 'defend the Revolution'. Later, in the same film, a clearly different platform can be seen to be in place in front of Miraflores on April 11. (Petition 1)

The filmmakers explained that when they realised in the edit that they were still short of material for one section of the film (the early part of the day on 11 April) to establish two different rallies, they chose to use a number of 'recent archive shots'.

We viewed this as legitimate reconstruction of key and factually true events and deployed this strongly representative and recent footage in a genuine attempt to assist the viewer toward an understanding of the nature of events on April 11.[1]

The total of recent archive footage used to flesh out the pre-coup crowd scenes is 47 seconds, of which the longest single segment is 19 seconds.

1.2 Opposition demonstration of 11 April 2002

In the same segment, the voice of the narrator says that '... very early, the opposition concentrated in Chuao...', but that text is edited with images of the opposition rally hours later, in another part of the city, where effectively the rally showed a greater pugnacity than at the beginning, although at no time were armed people seen. Indeed, to show the opposition rally, the filmmakers used only closed takes and horizontal angulations [sic] to avoid showing the gigantic magnitude of the rally, close to one million people, according to the abundant available audiovisual registries. (Petition 2)

A VHS tape was complied by the complainants to support these allegations. The filmmakers responded:

The statement of purpose and intent is entirely false. In any instance where recent archive footage was used, this was done in a genuine attempt to assist the viewer toward an understanding of events. All of the minimal recent archive deployed is used even-handedly between pro- and anti-Chávez crowds. None of the footage depicts or concerns incidents at the core of the coup narrative[2]... from the pro- and anti-Chávez marchers sequence even throughout the next 35 minutes of core coup events, all footage used in April 11, 12 and 13 is entirely contemporaneous actuality.[3]

However, the producers readily acknowledge in hindsight, that 'this attempt to provide illustrative material at a specific point in the documentary is problematic in terms of the presentation of contemporaneous actuality and raises issues which may outweigh the illustrative value of the footage used. This is being addressed in agreement with the commissioning broadcasters.'[4]

Misuse of 'archive footage' referred to with euphemisms like 'strongly representative' or 'illustrative'[5] footage by the filmmakers is, of course, not the same as actuality material and therefore breaks the codes of documentary representation. A case may be made for a film representing an essential truth rather than the detail of an actual moment, and the movement of footage within a documentary is common in most documentary editing processes. Shots of a crowd cheering a baseball match at one point may be redeployed as a reaction shot at a completely different game. Indeed, in describing his approach to editing the film, Ángel Hernández Zoido indicates his free and creative attitude to the material. But, as Kim Bartley and Donnacha Ó Briain quickly realised, shifting roughly equivalent footage can destabilise confidence in the codes of the genre and allow the entire film to be attacked as inaccurate. In the case of controversial political material in *The Revolution Will Not Be Televised*, minor infractions were magnified, described as false and manipulative in intent and became part of a bigger issue. In retrospect, the filmmakers recognised that these problems are particularly serious in a film 'which in part deals with the use of images and news information in the context of political power.'[6]

1.3 Upper-middle-class women undergoing self-defence instruction

The sequence of the neighbourhood meeting where upper-middle-class women are given instruction in self-defence and small arms was filmed in June, but presented as part of the lead up to the coup in April.

> Certain images were presented in the film as if they had happened be-fore April 11, 2002, when in reality they were filmed, without written con-sent, three months later. This is the case of a neighbors meeting held in June 2002, with the aim of preparing defensive actions in the face of the threats made by the government through its 'Bolivarian Circles' (groups of aggressive militants of the government's party who frequently attack the opposition rallies with stones, sticks and even gunshots) of attacking [sic] the housing estates of Caracas where the opposition predominates. These neighbors, almost all of them were women, received self-defense training from a voluntary instructor in order to learn to defend themselves – in June 2002 – from a presumed attack by the government support-ing groups. In the documentary being sponsored by you, that scene was edited and presented as if it had happened in January that year, as a part of the presumed '*coup d'état*' climate promoted by 'rich people' against Chávez. That scene, otherwise, gives a somber atmosphere and is preced-ed of [sic] a general view of the city at night and a luxurious building, as if to underscore the presumptuously subversive character of the meeting of 'ladies of the high society'. (Petition 7)

The phrasing of this section of the complaint also introduces extraneous explanations – a presumption on behalf of the women explaining why they might be threatened or attacked. The filmmakers responded, saying that this sequence was presented as part of 'the coup climate' since 'no causal link between the two events is offered or implied. The sequence is illustra-tive of social attitudes fundamental to Venezuelan politics and serves no other function in the film.'[7]

In this case, the filmmakers' response is beside the point – the sequence is indeed explanatory of the class divisions underlying the conflict and has a sharp satirical edge, but its placing in the film clearly deploys it as more than general background; it also becomes an illustration or explanation of the rising temperature of social conflict in Venezuela at that time. The remark by the instructor that 'it's important to keep an eye on domestic servants' exemplifies an assumed set of relationships between social groups and indicates the breakdown of a social order. Visually – bejewelled ladies denouncing the Chávez project – it goes beyond general social attitudes and becomes a key component in the explanation of the specific logic of the coup. Venezuelan sociologist Maria Pilar Garcia-Guadilla states: 'Much of the anti-democratic practices of intolerance and exclusion carried on by the opposition in general and specifically by their social organisations are grounded in social "fictions", which are in turn reinforced by the heightened social polarisation resulting from high indices of poverty as well as the political polarisation vis-á-vis the government of President Hugo Chávez. These fictions serve to justify actions of spatial and social exclusion of the "other".[8] The 'not in front of the servants' comment points to the intrusion of the subordinate 'other' in the safe space of the middle class.

But the indisputable implication of the chronological organisation of the film leads to the sequence being read as taking place *before* the coup in the succession of events. Of course it may be argued that, since the defence briefing is less of a punctual historical event or action and more of a background social indication, it *could* have happened at any point before or after the specific events of mid-April 2002. It is indicative behaviour within a social milieu which stretches before and after those events. Clearly that particular evening in June was not the first time that the emergency/self-defence instructor had opened his laptop to discourse about small arms.[9] But, most crucially, it breaks the style and grammar of a documentary organised chronologically and therefore undermines the credibility of the piece.

Obviously the sequence helps the explanatory logic early in the documentary, but this is not compatible with strict chronology. Perhaps the issue was not crucial, but it became a hostage to fortune and was seized upon when the film came under attack. Interestingly, 'interview with bourgeois – date' appears as a scribble on my notes of the rough cut viewing in November 2002, which may indicate that some issue of timing had arisen about the sequence at an early stage in post-production.

After receiving an early version of the critique, the BBC added a date caption for its second transmission.[10] This minor adjustment (an indication of defensive and evasive action, which became evident when the documentary was rebroadcast), was immediately interpreted by complainants in a triumphalist mode:

> In said broadcast, a detail was added: in the scene of the Neighbors Association, a title, that was not shown in any other previous version of the video: June 26, 2002. As this addition corresponds to the documented denounce [sic] that Mr Wolfgang Schalk presented before you in a letter dated on [sic] July 2003, it is evident that the versions of the film are being corrected in order to try to remedy the severe faults to information ethics that are being denounced by us. Regarding this point, we wish to say that these corrections only confirm the authenticity of our exposures and do not in any way diminish the responsibility of the directors, the producers and your TV Corporation in the misrepresentation of the historic truth of the events happened [sic] in Venezuela. We have enough copies of the videos broadcasted [sic] in different countries and by the BBC in the past, to confirm said statements. (Petition 8)

One can detect a smug glow of success in the complainants. Because they had made a point stick and revealed a weakness in the film's construction, they had, in their minds, forced a change which they could press forward to undermine the film as a whole.

In passing, the petition also asserts that the neighbourhood meeting was filmed without written consent. This is a dereliction of professional practice; the formality of signed 'consent forms' provides legal protection for both filmmakers and interviewees. Kim Bartley and Donnacha Ó Briain responded that written agreement had been given by the organiser of the meeting, the man delivering the lecture, and that verbal consent had been granted by the women at the session who voiced their adverse opinions of the government. But the lack of full formal, written consent from all involved is another minor vulnerability of the programme which came to light as those critical of it used all means to undermine it.[11]

OFCOM wrote to the producers in September 2005 indicating that the complaints made nearly two years earlier by three of the women interviewed in this sequence had not been upheld. They dismissed a complaint from one of the interviewees of unfair treatment and an unwarranted infringement of privacy:

> Mrs Fiorella Morales complained that she was misled as to the nature and purpose of the programme and that inclusion of footage of her in the programme gave a misleading impression of her. Also she complained that her privacy was unwarrantably infringed in the making and broadcast of the programme. OFCOM considered that reasonable steps were taken to inform Mrs Morales about the nature and purpose of the programme and noted that she had contributed freely and willingly. It also considered that Mrs Morales' views were not materially misrepresented in the programme and that it was unlikely that viewers would have been left with an unfair impression of her character. OFCOM considered that Mrs Morales' privacy was not infringed in either the making or broadcast of the programme. Mrs Morales was aware that she was being filmed and did not raise any objection at the time of filming.[12]

The adjudicating authority took a robust view of the construction of the sequence and the way in which the women were represented: 'OFCOM considered that it was unlikely that the editing of the programme would have materially affected viewers understanding of [the interviewees'] comments and, in our view, the programme's presentation of [their] comments was not unfair.'[13]

2. Detailed allegations of factual errors

2.1 Shooting from the bridge – the secrets of the shadows
The petition claimed that the version of events presented in the film – that the Chávez supporters filmed on the Llaguno Bridge were not firing their handguns in self-defence at snipers in the surrounding buildings, but were actually shooting at the opposition march – was false.

> The so-called 'case of the gun shooters on the Llaguno Bridge' is more complicated. Those who are not experts in audiovisual matters cannot have perceived what Wolfgang Schalk could notice and demonstrate. The

images of a group of President Chávez's supporters shooting from a bridge in the direction of the place where the opposition rally was coming [from] became famous (the journalistic team that took the images was awarded the King of Spain's Journalism Prize for this report). The film supported by you backed up the government 'propaganda version' that those people were not shooting at any rally, and for this, filmmakers used images from an amateur video taken from a different angle than the one used by the journalistic team that won the prize in Spain. In this second video, the bridge and the avenue underneath are completely empty, without persons or rally walking [sic] and no person shooting from the bridge. Using a 'shadow analysis' procedure similar to the ancient sun dials, Mr Schalk showed that the images of this amateur video were taken from about 1:00 to 1:30 in the afternoon, when the opposition rally was not even near that location, while the images taken by the prize-winning journalists were taken between 4:30 and 5:00 in the afternoon, when the tragic events were indeed happening. If the filmmakers had access to that amateur video, they could have also shown the images of the same place three hours later, when tens of people could be seen running and falling dead or injured in the same avenue, which was empty before. (Petition 5)

The filmmakers responded:

Our version is backed up by a wealth of documentary evidence, including that of numerous eyewitnesses on the day. These include, among others, the deputy editor of the French newspaper *Le Monde Diplomatique*,[14] who was present on the bridge that day. The evidence confirms that the men in question were indeed shooting in self-defence at sniper fire and at members of the pro-opposition Metropolitan Police.[15]

Two other films support the explanation offered by *The Revolution Will Not Be Televised*: the Australian television programme *Anatomy of a Coup* which was shown on the SBS channel,[16] and two years later another comprehensive documentary called *Puente Llaguno: Claves de una Masacre* (Llaguno Bridge: Clues of a Massacre) by Ángel Palacios which was screened at the Latin American Film Festival in Havana in December 2004. Both these films support the factual data and the claims contained in Bartley and Ó Briain's film. *Puente Llaguno* combines footage from different cameras to show that the 'shooters on the bridge' began firing 43 minutes after the last demonstrator had been hit.[17] Subsequently a Venezuelan court determined that four men who fired had been acting in self-defence, and Henry Vivas, Head of the Metropolitan Police testified that the opposition march did not arrive at Llaguno bridge. As the voice-over in *Puente Llaguno* suggests, 'all Venezuelans, no matter what political tendencies we belong to, were used as characters in the script of a *coup d'état* which required victims and assassins'. Perhaps the conjecture and shadow analysis 'similar to the ancient sundials' merely indicate the extraordinary determination to disprove any detail of the film.

It is also remarkable that a single image – that of a crouching man with a handgun apparently shooting in support of the government at opposition demonstrators – should have been seized upon and transmitted around the world as an explanation of why President Chávez had been obliged to resign. The visual image carries the connotations of unvarnished truth in a way that thousands of words do not, and it was this representation that the opponents of the regime needed to explain and consolidate their action. Its usage on international television, websites and the written media that day indicates how successful a single, iconic picture can be in creating emotion and affecting opinion. The immense power of the international image system is open to influence and manipulation from diverse political perspectives.

Cui bono arguments – understanding unexplained or unclaimed events by asking 'who benefits?' – should always be used warily. But the deadly operations of the snipers fit better within the unemotional logic of a coup plan, rather than as a tactic that would clearly be unhelpful to a government trying to stabilise the situation at that point. Circumstantial evidence, the degree of expertise necessary to carry out this action and the cold-blooded ability to annihilate civilian demonstrators of either side, would also point in the same direction.

In all the debate, let us not to forget the finality of the waste of innocent life that April day in Caracas. Whatever their politics, whether they were for or against Chávez, 19 citizens who were on the streets playing a role in their country's contemporary history were blown away without warning. 'War is simple', as Jean-Luc Godard once remarked; 'you take a piece of metal and put it in a piece of flesh.'[18]

2.2 President's alleged resignation

The petition alleges that Chávez had actually resigned at one point during the night of 12 April and that the documentary deliberately omitted this.

> The film insists that the President never resigned office. However, the military high command, lead by General in Chief Lucas Rincón, the main military officer and current Secretary of Domestic Affairs of Chávez, broadcasted [sic] a statement by radio and TV at 3:20 a.m. on the morning of April 12, in which he announced that (the) President 'was requested to resign office, which he agreed to'. This fact leads us to two possibilities: (1) either General Rincón stated a truth that was accepted throughout the whole country (as a matter of fact, after that information, the President surrendered peacefully at Fort Tiuna, a military base several kilometers away, without any physical threat and escorted by soldier friends and priests), or (2) that General Rincón lied, because he was an accomplice of a *coup d'état* (however, that seems not to be the truth, because he is still one of the main men of Chávez). This singular event, known by all Venezuelans and of undeniable importance to reconstruct [sic] what happened that day, was simply ignored by the filmmakers. They only edited the exit of the President from the palace and immediately thereafter the announcement of Pedro Carmona – at 04:50 a.m. of [sic] April 12 – of a new government. (Petition 4)

The filmmakers' response was a strong rebuttal that, although they agreed that General Lucas Rincón had indeed announced that Chávez 'had agreed to resign', crucially no evidence existed of an actual resignation. 'No document has ever been produced. It can be presumed that none ever existed.'[19] It may surely be presumed that if such a crucial document existed, it could play a significant role in appearing to legitimise the coup – the pro-coup activists would have used it extensively. In fact, the accession of Pedro Carmona to the presidency was extra-constitutional, as Article 233 of the Venezuelan Constitution requires that if a President resigns, his place is to be taken automatically by the Vice President, at that time Diosdado Cabello. Discussion of the details of resignation, wrote Roldan Tomasz Suárez, are 'nothing more than a smokescreen to cover up the simple and clear fact that Chávez Friás's resignation was never formalised according to procedure stipulated in the Constitution and therefore, such a resignation never materialised ... Even if he had been forced to sign under duress, the document would have no legal value at all' (2002).

Two contending narratives are at stake in these differing versions of events. The opposition was anxious to establish that Chávez had resigned voluntarily, had 'surrendered peacefully'; it is extraordinary that the complainants could assert that Chávez had been taken to Fort Tiuna 'without any physical threat'. In late 2002 and throughout 2003 the opposition's account was that there had been a 'vacuum of power' into which the new regime, led by Pedro Carmona, stepped, almost as an act of civic responsibility. The veracity of this account was an important issue in the lead-up to the recall referendum in August 2004.

The importance of this constitutional nicety was not lost on any of the participants – it is an indication of a desire for legitimacy in the middle of the messy, confused hiatus that took place on the night of the attempted coup. The film reveals the specific military pressure on Chávez to resign, the discussions with military officers in a closed room, and reveals the alacrity with which the new regime abolished the National Assembly and the Supreme Court, and dismissed the Head of the Central Bank, the Ombudsman and the Attorney General the next day. This is also an issue in international reporting. Greg Palast, who reports for the *Observer* and the BBC, suggests a source of the fallacious allegations: 'Who was the source of this "resignation" lie? I asked a US reporter why American news media had reported this nonsense as stone fact without checking. The reply was that it came from a reliable source: "we got it from the State Department"' (2003: 13).

Whatever the version of the sequence of events on 11 April, there is no basis for overturning a previous democratic process and forcing the resignation of a democratically elected politician. The niceties of formal resignation are almost beside the point when considering the level of duress that had been exerted in subverting the democratic and legal process.

2.3 Tanks on the street/Plan Ávila

The petition suggests that the documentary voice-over deliberately and misleadingly referred to military tanks surrounding the Presidential Palace of Miraflores as part of the pressure being brought to bear by the dissident military in order to persuade the President to resign office.

In order to secure their thesis of a military *coup d'état* on April 11, the commentator voice of the documentary refers to some military tanks 'surrounding the Presidential Palace of Miraflores as a pressure step for the President to resign office'; simultaneously, the image shows them briefly, parked inside the Presidential Palace. In the version presented by NPS in the Netherlands they are shown longer [sic], in the proper introduction of the film, while they advance on the highway, an image that was omitted in the Venezuelan version. In reality the presence of these armored cars on the streets was due to an order given by President Chávez to his military chiefs in order to apply the so called 'Ávila Plan', a military operation consisting in [sic] the military forces acting to repress thousands of civilians that were on the streets at that time of the day. This fact is documented by a record of [the] internal radio circuit of the army and was publicly acknowledged by Chávez in the days after April 13. Chávez's order was disobeyed by most of the generals and troop commanders, to avoid a terrifying massacre as a consequence of the attack of armored troops against unarmed civilians and they ordered the tank column to return to the military base. Most of them stopped and went back to the barracks, but a group of 4 tanks went on to the Presidential Palace supporting the President; the doors were opened and they were parked there as fire power supporting Chávez. By the way, this disobedience of the generals – outraged in view of the mass murder that happened earlier that day in the surroundings of the Presidential Palace – was the cause of the authority crisis that – hours later – led to the resignation of Chávez and his peaceful surrender to the military chiefs, a complex problem that the government and the documentary simplify as a classical Latin American 'coup d'état'. You will understand the coarse inversion in the narration of the facts that this means. The filmmakers simply narrated the facts totally back to front of how [sic] they actually happened, omitting such crucial – and newsy

– facts as the long record of the radio communications between Chávez and several of his generals in a moment of extremely serious tension and national security crisis. (Petition 14)

The filmmakers made this rejoinder:

For reasons unexplained, the complainant falsely quotes the voice-over. The voice-over in fact says: 'We could see on TV that the palace had been surrounded by tanks.' Many high-ranking military had already come out against Chávez, when the news that tanks were coming reached the palace. This caused fear and confusion within the Palace.[20]

Actually the voice-over also carries the same implication – that the armoured vehicles were hostile – but the filmmakers' point represented the understandable, albeit confused, perception in the palace that night. There were also allegations from Lucia Astier,[21] a Venezuelan filmmaker based in Europe, that the film's reference to the air force threatening a deadline to bomb the palace was not practical or realistic:

It is also a fact that even if the threat of bombardment was true, there was no way of carrying out the threat. The Venezuelan air force, like all Latin American air forces, does not have the capability to bomb a building in the centre of town. It doesn't matter what the Chávistas were telling you on the night, the filmmakers had months of editing to check their facts and demonstrate a little curiosity about simple journalistic queries such as security in buildings surrounding the palace, etc or who controlled the tanks. This should have happened during the edit process...[22]

But the perceived threat of force, even if can be argued to be a bluff, still constitutes a breach of the democratic process; it is still a threat of the use of force to achieve extra-constitutional aims.

The confused versions of events occurred in a situation in which wild rumours and speculation were circulating at high velocity. Perhaps recalling images from the memory of the bombing of the Presidential Palace in Santiago, Chile, during the coup against Salvador Allende on 11 September

1973, the people in the palace took the threat seriously. The argument taking place here is a political one, but it is also an argument between different styles of filmmaking: *cinéma vérité* focuses on the representation of the powerful emotions engendered during the moment of crisis; and a cooler and more distant style of filmmaking in which the final analysis, corrected with historical hindsights, is laid out in voice-over and interview.

Plan Ávila was a contingency plan to deploy the armed forces in the face of a threat to public order: the army takes over strategic services and occupies sites of importance for the maintenance of essential public services. In principle, the plan is one for security and prevention only and is misconstrued in the complainants' formulation: 'a military operation … to repress thousands of civilians'. The transcription of a supposed conversation between Chávez and other military commanders on the Globovision website[23] is insightful: the clean, clear military evaluation of the current circumstances (a 'SITREP' – 'situation report' in military jargon), and decisive deployments made to meet it, shows the calm and precise operation of military practices in a moment of danger.

The absence of details and arguments about the abortive Plan Ávila also depends on selection priorities in the construction of the film. At the late stage of post-production most of the work is focused on what material should be left out, especially when you have 199 hours to discard in order to make a 74-minute feature-length documentary.

3. Representation of the opposition

The petition initiated a substantial debate about the way in which the film represented the complexion of the opposition to Chávez; the racial and class make-up of the opposition as evidenced by the demonstrators on the streets, but also the women receiving self-defence training, media pundits and television presenters. Put most baldly, the petition's critique argues that the documentary's representation of the political divide in Venezuela as one based on class and racial conflict is flawed.

Critics of the film were determined to stress that 'the political problem of Venezuela does not consist of the class or racial confrontation … but the confrontation between the democratic aspiration of the majority and the dictatorial project which the government is trying to impose on us' (petition 13).

The filmmakers responded that 'while there are undoubtedly layers and nuances to the polarisation, all serious commentators broadly concur that Venezuela is split along economic – and racial – lines, and that the political situation reflects this. This was particularly pronounced at the time the documentary was made.'[24]

The petition was concerned that the documentary had intentionally distorted reality to represent the opposition marches as made up of a majority of white, middle-class citizens, when in fact 'these marches are predominantly made up of poor, and mixed race people' (petition 13). The filmmakers' response was robust: 'Opposition marches at the time the documentary was made were certainly not made up predominantly of poor, mixed-race Venezuelans.'[25] Perhaps unsurprisingly, polling in the lead-up to the referendum of 2004 suggested that the poor, who can be said to make up 65 per cent of Venezuelan society,[26] were more than twice as inclined to support Chávez as the rest of society, a finding that was consistent with past polls and election results (see Delacour 2004).

Issues of the composition and social range of their support base are clearly very important from the opposition's point of view. They are anxious to assert that the conflict should not be identified as a clash of social groups. In particular they are concerned that the anti-Chávistas are not seen as representing the selfish interests of a single class, but of 'Venezuela' as a whole. They wish to reconstitute the imaginary of the united nation in the face of the Chávistas' divisive interpretation of Venezuelan history: that heretofore control of wealth and power had been in the hands of a small oligarchy and that this had led to a severe economic division which was only now being redressed by policies of redistribution initiated by a socially progressive regime.

The effects of equivalent ideological conjuring tricks have permeated current discourses and institutions: those who contest the dominance of the bourgeoisie, a class which strives to achieve invisibility, find themselves shadow-boxing. As French critic Roland Barthes showed in his seminal *Mythologies* (1973), the bourgeoisie constantly achieves invisibility by naturalising its presence and perspective. It removes its own role and existence without trace. This modest self-effacement also manifests itself in various unconscious ideological assumptions that circulate in everyday opinion or doxa: it is natural that black people are better at dancing than mathematics and that women are better carers than car drivers. This is the inevitability of *the way things are*. All these issues, and the relationships that underpin them, are thus removed from rationality and taken into myth. Politics is itself depoliticised, evacuated, taken out of negotiation. 'It is when history is denied', as Barthes wrote, 'that it is most unmistakably at work' (1977b: 2).

Chávez's brand of radical nationalism had managed to displace the previous imaginary of the nation and extend it to wider social and racial groups. He had captured history (redeploying the figures of Simón Bolívar and Simón Rodríguez) and replaced the old idea of the nation with a more egalitarian one. The opposition sought to shift the basis of the argument to other grounds. Evidently it is easier to win a debate set in the clear-cut terms of 'democracy vs. dictatorship' than in the contentious terrain of arguments about the social division of wealth and power.

When Phil Gunson repeated the accusation that the filmmakers had represented the opposition too narrowly in the *Columbia Journalism Review* (2004a), they rebutted the assertion: 'The idea that Chávez supporters in 2002 were broadly poor and dark-skinned and the opposition broadly white and middle-class may seem simplistic but it's one we share with a number of commentators including the *Guardian* newspaper,[27] Professor Dan Hellinger of Webster University in Missouri, and indeed Gunson himself in *The Christian Science Monitor*.'[28] Greg Palast describes the contrast succinctly in the *Observer*: 'Look at the *San Francisco Chronicle*/AP photo of the anti-Chávez marchers and note their colour. White. And not just any white. A creamy *rich* white … And the colour of the *pro-Chávez* marchers? Dark brown. Brown and round as cola nuts' (2003: 13).

In a sense these demographic arguments came to a head when the recall referendum took place on 18 August 2004, for which all social groups had been mobilised in a protracted and polarised debate. The referendum was monitored by international and independent observers and the result showed that 58 per cent of the population continued to support Chávez; this represented a small increase on the 56 per cent of the first election in December 1998. In the subsequent presidential election held in December 2006 the Chávez vote was 63 per cent of the total.

4. Verbal formulations

The end credits include a 'where are they now' sequence, and the petition argued that while

> …the film says that 'Pedro Carmona fled to Colombia and a little later appeared in Miami…'. The truth is that Mr Carmona was arrested on the same April 13 and he was interpellated some days later by the Venezuelan Congress. Later, he was detained in his house for several days and then he took refuge in the Embassy of Colombia, a country which conceded him diplomatic asylum, which was accepted by the Venezuelan government, when conceding the respective safe-conduct; in May, Carmona traveled to Colombia, where he pursues his profession at the view of everybody [sic]… It is then clear that Carmona did neither 'flee' to Colombia as a delinquent, nor did he 'appear' a little later in Miami, as if he were an Osama Bin Laden whose whereabouts no one knows. (Petition 15)

While the tone of the end credit sequence is deliberately tongue-in-cheek, the details are accurate. It is reasonable to describe Pedro Carmona as 'fleeing' and 'appearing' in exile. This complaint only indicates the degree of detail in which the complainants became interested, and in the context of the attacks on the film, points that worried already jittery television executives.

5. Government complicity with the film – guilt by association

That Chávez had co-operated in the making of the project and, at a later date, took the finished film up as evidence of his version of events is understood by the petition writers as proof that there is continuity and complicity between the film and the regime. The petition suggests that

> *The Revolution Will Not Be Televised* is being presented … as an author's film, as an objective journalistic research film, while it is really a very good plotted [sic] and accomplished propaganda operation, supported logistically by the Venezuelan government, with the aim of misleading unprepared spectators of countries who do not know the totality of the referred events. (Petition 18)

Kim Bartley and Donnacha Ó Briain describe their position:

> It is clear that our sympathies are closer to the Chávez camp than to the Venezuelan opposition as we experienced it during our time in Venezuela. This point of view is perfectly reasonable in what is an authorial creative documentary and should be evident to any reasonable viewer. The documentary clearly displays other opposing points of view, which allow the viewer to make his or her own judgement about the events depicted.[29]

To what degree do 'other opposing points of view' really feature in the film? Specious and biased television commentators and the risible fury of the upper-middle-class women do not constitute a full or articulate political critique of Chávez. The film is made within a *vérité* genre and is not a vehicle for extensive analytical exposition or dialectical debate.

The film had been made independently, but because the Venezuelan state television used a digibeta copy (VTV had been given a copy since they had provided access to their archive) to duplicate the film and then use the cassettes directly and politically, this action could be perceived as undermining the independence and integrity of the documentary. Although the filmmakers cannot control such usage, it compromised the independence and political objectivity of the film – a problem for the discourses of 'impartial' broadcasting. In fact, they note somewhat wearily that 'so far, both sides of the political divide in Venezuela have used and abused the documentary to further their individual political battles.'[30]

When I was at Channel 4, there was a strong debate at a key weekly meeting called Programme Review (a forum where commissioning editors would discuss editorial matters and recent programmes) about a programme called *My Ireland* (1985) executive-produced by John Kelleher and directed by Michele Kurland. It depicted the then Taoiseach, Charles Haughey, displaying his role in his country with supreme confidence. He strides in front of the camera introducing the audience to his stud farm, his Gandon mansion, his island Inis Mhiceálláin, and he walks up to the border in Crossmaglen to 'play the green card' and denounce the division of the island of Ireland. At the Programme Review meeting Channel 4 editors were concerned that this was in fact merely an extended 'PPB' (Party Political Broadcast) without the proper independent critical editorial enquiry. John Ranelagh, the commissioning editor responsible, reminded the group that the Republic of Ireland was not in the same jurisdiction and therefore not subject to the same rules of balance as UK political programmes. For good measure, in a passing gratuitous sideswipe, he cited me and my colleague Alan Fountain (at that time in charge of the Independent Film and Video Department) for allegedly commissioning too many hagiographic programmes about Che Guevara! The argument was neatly resolved, however, when Seamus Cassidy (Commissioning Editor for Youth, originally from Derry) said that he understood that Haughey had duplicated copies of the programme and was selling cassettes to the faithful at the Fianna Fáil Árd Fheis (party conference) for £5 a copy. Not only was this a gross breach of copyright and legality, it also confirmed the suspicions of political cosiness and contiguity.

If a programme is produced independently its direct political use by those protagonists involved does not constitute a political contamination or guilt by association. After all, an assertion that the coup attempt was wrong and unsupportable may or may not lead to a belief that Chávez's political policies are right. This slippage from criticism of the coup to longerterm, more general support for a regime unjustly attacked is of course one that Chávez supporters work to encourage. Andy Goodall writes on the website of Venezuela Solidarity UK: 'An absolute must-see documentary. It details the story of the Coup from INSIDE the palace – the single biggest tool to prove the lies of the Venezuelan opposition.'[31]

However the Venezuelan and Cuban governments' distribution and usage of the finished film does indicate the correspondence of political perspectives and offers an angle of attack to those predisposed to its denunciation.

IN PROPORTION

The consistency and integrity of the representation is crucial to the politics of its message. Ethical questions loom large in any documentary, in the 'honesty' of its selection of interviewees and its editing of sequences, its construction and detail. Leaving aside the principled arguments, minor infractions of chronological and documentary logic (as this film so clearly shows) become hostages to fortune when such a film comes under sustained scrutiny and attack. In taking an extensive view of *The Revolution Will Not Be Televised*, we need to place the details of the critique of its significa-tion in proportionate relation to the overall picture. There is an old saying 'The devil is in the detail',[32] but this has to be set with due proportionality in relation to the overall context and response.

By and large, the film has been well-received by international, open-minded audiences. But behind the word 'open' is the insularity of the West, which often means little or no knowledge of most of the rest of the (Third) World or even, say, basic information about Latin American politics. But this raises the degree of over-determination any audience/viewer brings to a viewing as is illustrated by the most starkly and determinedly negative reaction the film encountered when it was shown to a small Venezuelan audience antipathetic to Chávez. The article Michael McCaughan wrote in the *Irish Times* (2003) following this exercise indicates the way that those closer to the situation carry their disapproving attitudes into a viewing of the film.

Robust criticism of a documentary like *The Revolution Will Not Be Tele-vised* can be characterised as part of the normal and predictable response in the antagonism of representations, the battle for meanings in the social domain. As Jonathan Swift once wrote with impeccable irony 'I must com-plain the cards are ill-shuffled 'till I have a good hand.' Alternatively, some have asserted that romantic European leftists, isolated and embattled in their own polity, always would-be 'tourists of the revolution' in distant do-mains, might seize upon this film as a simple cathartic experience which confirms their desire for an image of radical politics, far away (see Enzens-berger 1976b). 'Revolution is the opium of the intellectuals', is a slogan in Lindsay Anderson's *O Lucky Man!* (1973). And as Jean-Francois Revel put it, 'throughout history, men have projected on distant countries their politi-cal dreams or have gone with their dreams to those countries' (quoted in Gunson 2004b: 31). Purity and simplicity may be preserved by distance, but that does not justify the presupposition and figuration of scorn that en-ables those who oppose Chávez to account for foreigners that support him by dismissing them outright.

Standing back from *The Revolution Will Not Be Televised*, it does not seem sensible to try to reduce or eliminate the perspectives we carry to any viewing – the 'd'ou je parle' ('from where I speak') of our own determinations, which always traverse our readings of any given text or film anyway – but rather to bring them into reflective consciousness as part of a more reflexive debate.

ENDGAME

Arguments about the documentary continue on the Internet; postings on the film's message board on the Internet Movie Data Base (IMDb) include furious debate in 2005 and 2006. Wikipedia, an online encyclopaedia created by collective contributions, links *The Revolution Will Not Be Televised* to a blog created in August 2005 offering an analysis of the film 'three years after its release'. The critique reiterates most of the arguments of the original petition, but adds a stop-frame image of a presumably Venezuelan camera operator caught in a mirror in the Presidential Palace at the height of the coup who is clearly 'neither of the authors of the documentary'. The alleged implication is that the government were complicit in the making of the film.[33] The 81-minute documentary *X-Ray of a Lie* has been accessible since 13 June 2006 via Google Video; it begins with the repeated fabrication that on 11 April 2002 'demonstrators were attacked by Chávez supporters and the National Guard'.

In September 2005 OFCOM reported that as a result of the BBC's internal process a provisional adjudication of the complaints made by Adriana Vigilanza, Fiorella Morales and Aloma Henriquez (individuals interviewed during the neighbourhood meeting for self-defence instruction) were not upheld.[34] A month later the BBC Editorial Complaints Unit wrote to explain that they had closed down all other complaints connected with *The Revolution Will Not Be Televised* which had been made to what was then the Programme Complaints Unit, currently the Editorial Complaints Unit, and OFCOM would not be pursuing other criticisms of the programme.

REFLECTIONS

Credo quia incredibile.
I believe it because it is unbelievable.

The Revolution Will Not Be Televised raises questions of relevance to both documentary-making and understanding, and inevitably the complex politics of the particular histories it became part of. There are specific intersections between some of the formal constructions of the film and its political meanings and effects. Fictional and non-fictional forms are enmeshed in one another; the cinematic syntax and narrative construction often found in fiction films are constantly deployed in documentary genres to narrativise the real. The choice of a *cinéma vérité* style and a simple, classical narrative structure were discernible factors in this film's reception, although its impact should be seen in the continuing context of other reportage in Venezuela and internationally.

STORY STRUCTURE

A crucial and understated factor in the success of this remarkable film is how the subject and underlying structure of the narrative deliver a powerful dramatic experience and the 'word of mouth' of audiences and critical reviews report the pleasures of experiencing the film almost independently of its political meanings. This is a result of the simple tripartite narrative structure that underlies conventional storytelling, and which is in place here:

Exposition

Jeopardy

Redemption

Mick Eaton, a successful screenwriter (and once a student of anthropology), explained that this structure may be extended to myth and underlies the form of all human ritual:

> In so called primitive societies you find the basic process of ritual moving through three stages: a young boy is introduced, goes through a ceremony and then becomes a warrior. A couple are presented, a ritual takes place and then they are married. A dead person is laid to rest, there is a ceremony and their spirit is released.[1]

In the last decade the attention to story structure which had been initiated by the Russian Formalists eighty years earlier has been revived through the extraordinary expansion of vocational courses for screenwriters. The pioneering work of Vladimir Propp in *The Morphology of the Folktale*, written in 1922, examined the motifs and recurrent patterns in hundreds of European folk stories. Just after World War Two, Joseph Campbell's *The Hero with a Thousand Faces* (1949) brought an anthropological and Jungian approach to myths and legends; this work was taken to the commercial market for screenwriting by Christopher Vogler in *The Writer's Journey* (first published in 1992), subtitled 'Mythic Structure for Writers' and, most notoriously, in the dogmatic formulations of Robert McKee in *Story* (1999). The commercial drive in present-day film production resulted in a greater concentration on the development stage and script-editing; this has encouraged a formulaic approach to narrative structure in screenplay writing. Although these perspectives are rarely applied to documentary-making, the same structures of storytelling are relevant and *The Revolution Will Not Be Televised* exemplifies the power of their successful enactment.

Even if they were not intended as such, the film's final sequences – the returning President's descent from the night sky in a helicopter – can be interpreted in some sense as a scene where the saviour returns to earth.[2] One could even suggest that the timescale also offered a certain messianic metaphor because Hugo Chávez was deposed on a Friday, only to return in a miraculous political resurrection on the following Sunday. Even General Jorge García Carneiro deploys religious terminology to describe it as 'the day of civil-military union and of national resurrection' (in Guevara 2005: 138). Here we can see the contingent disposition of events, their configurations having certain iconic resonance entirely unintended by the filmmakers. These are the circumstances that by chance (rather than conscious human intention or intervention) fall into patterns of visual representation which correspond to culturally pre-existent meanings.

THE SOUND OF MUSIC

However, it is a combination of its underlying narrative structure and the deployment of both on- and off-screen music which finally brings our emotions into play as we watch the film.

Although it was never raised by any of the complainants, the use of music recalls the questions that Hanns Eisner and Theodor Adorno raised in their book *Composing for the Films* (1947) and that Kurt London had already cited in *Film Music* (1936), to 'drag film music out of the dark shadows of illusion into the limelight of general discussion and enquiry'. As one of the most persuasive and yet invisible elements in film and television programmes, the use of music as a rhythmic undercarriage to the action and an emotional trigger tends to support the unconscious reception of a film's meaning. Music is also a significant factor in delivering emotions and feelings at specific points in story structure (see Garratt & Stoneman 1982). The remarkable similarities of musical organisation in 'fiction' and 'documentary' point to the parallel forms of narrative construction in both genres.

In *The Revolution Will Not Be Televised*, montage sequences introduce music with a carefully contrived unobtrusiveness; ominous chords are played under the first appearance of Carmona and Ortega. The on-screen music made by pro-Chávez demonstrators generates positive and dramatic build-up. But the combination of image and music in these sequences, while it can pejoratively be described as 'manipulative', can also be seen as the normal work of documentary filmmaking – to articulate all the elements of sound and image in their most direct, co-ordinated and persuasive form.

THE NATURE OF *CINÉMA VÉRITÉ*: THE LIMITS OF THE VISIBLE

This version of the *vérité* documentary genre exemplifies all the strengths and the limitations of that form in general, which are also heightened by the film's overtly political subject matter. Although it is combined with reportage, especially in the introductory sections, the *vérité* mode of the long mid-section in the palace takes us closer to the 'reality effect' of the drama, but it also inevitably limits discursive analysis and excludes attention to external factors. Those who look to this film for an extensive exposition and exploration of the context and complexity of political change in Venezuela are looking for a different kind of film.[3]

For example, it has been said that the film does not reflect what was really going on during the days following the coup, that it oversimplifies events and leaves out the complex recalibration of the equilibrium of power inside the military. There had been an open rebellion from sections of the High Command, which clearly had led to a situation in which either they would have to resign or they would have to force the President to resign. In the ensuing turmoil, it was inevitable that there were hours of weighing the strength of the various factions (institutional, Chávistas and anti-Chávistas). This was not happening inside the Miraflores palace, however, but in Fort Tuina and other military bases throughout the country.[4] Hugo Chávez did not need to have a gun pointed at his head to know that he did not have full control of the armed forces at that moment.

As Lucia Astier explains:

For the Venezuelan armed forces fighting among themselves is very problematic as they are a very insular group, socially they come from the middle classes all the way down to campesinos and the presence of the upper-middle classes is rare. There is some implicit sense of the military 'family', sometimes literally since they know each other socially, they are married to the daughter of that general and that other lieutenant. At some level the armed forces in Venezuela is a relatively egalitarian institution with a strong awareness of community.[5]

One can speculate that loyalty to Chávez is a combination of recognition that he is 'one of ours', some elements of conscious political support and enthusiasm for his use and positioning of the army in civil society. Many senior officers had been given positions of power in civilian institutions as the armed forces were deployed to take a central role in the process of social transformation.

It is likely that the forces for and against the coup and the non-aligned institutional factions within the armed forces were still negotiating when Pedro Carmona and his associates overplayed their hand and announced the disbandment of the National Assembly, the Supreme Tribunal and other democratic institutions. At that point, the non-aligned institutional officers, and in particular General Baduel (who controlled the airbase that held the F-16s), broke ranks. The High Command was forced to withdraw support from Carmona and, eventually, the balance of power moved back towards the Chávista loyalists. The presence of Chávez supporters on the street strengthened their hand and in the end the High Command had to accept defeat and bring back Chávez. It was a very fluid situation and could have gone either way.

General Jorge García Carneiro gives an insightful account of the dynamic of the military hierarchy, indicating that many switched their support back to the President because they were disappointed that they had not received the promotions they were expecting from the Carmona group: for instance, 'General Vázquez Velazco was obviously deeply embittered that he had supported the *coup d'état* but had not received the post he had hoped for' (in Guevara 2005: 134). A key person in this moment of jeopardy is General Lucas Rincón, who announced Chávez's resignation at 3.20 a.m. on national television, but on Chávez's return was made Minister of Defence and eventually became Minister of the Interior.

In what way does the *invisibility* of the flux of these negotiations constitute a gap or lacuna in the account of events given in *The Revolution Will Not Be Televised*? Even though it cannot show what is going on in private discussions behind the scenes, within the genre of *cinéma vérité* the film indicates the main areas of activity on the day – those crucial swings in state and popular power.

An early sequence of the film – showing Chávez arriving at Miraflores and bestowing a comradely embrace on a palace sentry – was a subtle, understated indicator of his attention to a close relationship with the palace guard and by extension to the military which, in the end, was crucial to the reconstitution of his power. While the internal military 'consultations' cannot be shown, the rapid movement of soldiers to retake the palace (which was surrounded by protesters) represents the combined action of the armed forces and Chávistas on the street, which resulted in the coup reversal on 14 April.

As a genre, *cinéma vérité* can have undoubted emotional power, but it is not a form well suited to a great depth of reflective examination or political analysis. Donnacha Ó Briain acknowledges that there is 'a rational and justifiable criticism here: you have choices when you make documentaries; we had a certain type of footage – it sustains an emotional response, living through a chaotic and highly affecting event that changed all of us quite profoundly … For me, anyway, to argue for *vérité* is not to suggest that it's more truthful; really it's more direct, a more powerful short circuit to the emotional.'

The emotional and narrative experience, however, does add up to a form of analysis and a new understanding; when you see the succession of events chronologically, a whole orchestrated shape emerges. Putting events together to reveal their organisation has a different and more significant impact than isolated fragments of information. The separate events add up to a planned approach. This is confirmed by the pivotal extracts from a television chat show where, the morning after the coup, participants explicitly boasted of their involvement: 'The General's video statement was made to make Chávez stay in Venezuela, because Chávez had a trip planned to Costa Rica and we needed him here for the plan to work. So then Chávez stayed here and we activated the plan.'[6] For many people in Venezuela, the film made it clear that a concerted attempt at a *coup d'état* had actually been perpetrated and that, following its failure, one side had attempted to rewrite history.

A SHORT HISTORY OF POLITICAL DOCUMENTARY

Academic discourses which have grown up over the last two decades to surround the documentary film are also relevant to understandings of *The Revolution Will Not Be Televised*. They provide an intellectual framework

which feeds into the debates which surround the categorisations of particular films as fiction or non-fiction, and they underlie some of the controver-
sies and contestations that took place around Bartley and Ó Briain's film.

The documentary genre is defined not by a formal strategy, but by its
claim to a certain relation to reality and truth. Like all forms of film, it is
entirely constructed; however, unlike other genres a great deal more is at
stake in the way in which this construction negotiates real events. There is
always a high degree of selection and manipulation in the materials of its
manufacture, but these processes of fabrication involved in a film, or any
other cultural artefact, do not mean that it is untrue. That the truth is relative
and perspectival does not mean that *there is no truth*.

Subtle differences emerge in the degree to which different forms of
documentary film efface or foreground this process of fabrication for the
viewer, and the style of *vérité* works to smooth away the particular articula-
tion of the real events it depicts without trace.

The critique which headed the Internet petition against the film challenged the arguments the filmmakers made for the redeployment of
'archive' footage as 'illustrative'. The break in the otherwise chronological ordering of events depicted in the film, when the sequence showing
the upper-middle-class women undergoing self-defence instruction was
placed before the coup, became a difficult issue for the filmmakers. Even if
those mounting the critique of the film did not utilise the terms of debate
developed in the widening institutional spaces of academic film studies,
their arguments came from an implicit understanding of the codes that
structure documentary films.

Kim Bartley and Donnacha Ó Briain describe their film as 'an authorial
creative documentary' and indeed it exemplifies the contemporary prolifer-
ation of more hybrid combinations of non-fiction forms: exposition is combined with interviews, observation with performance, *vérité* with film clips
used as quotation. The 'creative arrangement of actuality'[7] of documentary
and the imaginative recordings of fiction do not stand in simple binary opposition to one another; even if we use the term everyday to categorise and
separate the audio-visual, documentary is more a place where the genres
and languages of film co-habit and interact. As Paul Ward observes, 'it is in
the dialectical progression and hybridising of these categories – where a

purely observational style meets a more interview-heavy, reflexive style for instance – that innovations are made' (2005: 13).

There are several areas of filmmaking that deliberately work across the separation of the documentary/fiction categories. An extraordinary sequence in Haskell Wexler's *Medium Cool* (1969) occurs when its protagonist, a journalist helpfully wearing a visually prominent yellow dress, steps into the 1968 Democratic convention in Chicago and finds herself in the middle of Mayor Daly's police riot. A 'fictional' character moves through a situation that is a long way beyond the control of the filmmaker. *Requiem for Dominic* (Robert Dornhelm, 1990) plays a drama amongst the collapse of the Ceacescu regime in Romania. Or, more recently, *Sous les Bombes* (*Under the Bombs*) by Philippe Aractingi (2007) takes his protagonists into southern Lebanon in the days at the end of the Israeli invasion in July 2006. Less dramatic historical events provide the backdrop to a long hybrid project I was involved in commissioning at Channel 4: *Route One* (Robert Kramer, 1990) which encountered contemporary America by taking an actor in a semi-fictional role down the highway which spans from Canada to Florida.

The terms of political documentary production that had developed between the world wars (especially during the Spanish Civil War) were recast by the shift after World War Two to new forms of documentary made possible by increasingly portable equipment – *cinéma vérité* in France and Direct Cinema in the United States. Ironically the French label derived from Dziga Vertov's *Kino Pravda*, a much more politicised version of early documentary aesthetic in which the codes are made more visible; mediational structures are constructed as formative rather than mere embellishments.[8] Something of this greater reflexivity also carried through to the French documentary movement. This is indicated in Edgar Morin's formulation, given at an event on *cinéma vérité* at the Pompidou Centre in Paris: 'There are two ways to conceive of the cinema of the real. The first is to pretend that you can present reality to be seen; the second is to pose the problem of reality. In the same way, there are two ways to conceive *cinéma vérité*. The first is to pretend that you bring truth; the second is to pose the problem of truth.'

These developments in filmmaking are transformed in the institutional placement of non-fiction within the popular media. The gradual predominance of variations on *cinéma vérité* in recent years is connected with the spread of Reality TV formats; this has strengthened the use of the genre in factual and news production. *Cinéma vérité* has skewed expectations and created fraudulent terms which, in its notional neutrality, effaced the personal and political dimensions in factual filmmaking. Television regulatory structures recast aspects of documentary form in relation to veracity and balance; for factual formats this led to the absorption and transformation of those traditions of overtly politicised usage of documentary. They were subjected to new regulatory structures which institutionally defined the grammar of documentary filmmaking in a way which reinforced the ideology of unmediated truth, the journalistic ethic of non-intervention and strict observation (see Winston 2000: 90).

The meanings created within documentary processes inevitably inhabit the domain of politics, but there are further questions about how evident those processes are to spectators and what response is encouraged by the form of a given film. Do the extended duration of single shots in Amos Gitai's *Field Diary* (1982) and *Pineapple* (1984) 'show themselves showing'? Do Nick Broomfield and Michael Moore's pronounced performance of their documentary enquiries bring their process into focus? Whilst *The Revolution Will Not Be Televised* does not work to foreground its constructive process it does arguably stimulate the starting point of active engagements. 'Artwork should encourage inquiry, offer space for judgement, and provide the tools for evaluation and further action – in short, encourage an active response' (Winston 2000: 31).

But the meticulous scholarly delineation of the hybrid genres of documentary form is a long way from contention in a television context. The nuances of academic documentary courses and conferences, scholarly publications and intellectual discourses do not connect with the perceptions of either the public or of powerful institutions that control public media.

A MOST DISINGENUOUS GENRE

Vérité is a sub-category of the larger genre of documentary. Our expectations of 'documentary' arise from its differentiation from 'fiction'. Although the assumed basis for this dichotomy allows it to be deployed frequently, there is actually a more contradictory blurring between the two categories. Jean-Luc Godard's disingenuous quip in *Éloge de l'amour* (*In Praise of Love*, 2001), 'I don't understand the word documentary', points towards the highly permeable boundaries around these categories of filmmaking. The ideas about the 'objective reality' implicit in photography and film that André Bazin developed in *Cahiers du cinéma*, a magazine Godard joined in the early 1950s, would have made him conscious of the paradoxes whereby a fiction feature records actual actors standing in front of specific landscapes, and a continuous hand-held synch-sound shot in a *vérité* documentary selects and constructs its meanings. Experimental filmmaker Malcolm LeGrice takes a categorical view: 'A documentary is not a document. Documentaries try to fit the factual inside a narrative and that's always problematic. Documentary puts a pattern on something that invariably becomes false as a result of the narrativisation.' It has a predisposition towards certain forms of signification: 'It excludes doubt. The film image, in the strength of its presence, doesn't have a questioning mode. Its apparent present reduces hesitancy, uncertainty, speculation.'[9]

In relation to the versions of documentary form, *vérité* effaces its own operations in the most thoroughgoing mode. Its codes work to achieve 'the reality effect' effacing themselves as part of a guarantee of veracity. In Donnacha Ó Briain's telling comment: 'It's the visceral crackle that is there with *vérité*, the sequences which tell their own story.' It is in the phrase 'tell their own story' that the effacement of the filmmaking process occurs.

This was also true for Ángel Hernández Zoido when editing the film:

> I particularly remember the rushes of the snipers over the bridge. We had the material recorded by Kim and Donnacha: people being shot from the roofs of the surrounding buildings, the paramedics inside the palace carrying injured people and the National Guards trying to find out the direction of the fire. I remember their faces when nobody knew what was really happening. I could feel the fear of being attacked by a hidden enemy. But we also had some tapes from other people in different places around the bridge. I remember the images were so 'real' that I was really impressed. I've edited firing scenes in fiction films many times. Actors generally use fake guns and you have to add the sounds of the detonation, the bullets whistling and the impacts in different soundtracks to be mixed later. Even

in documentaries, like one I edited where there's a sequence about the Vietnam War, I've used a lot of file material usually mute or previously edited with music, library sounds and voice-over. But when I cut the scene of the snipers I only used the real sound. Perhaps for the audience there's no difference but it was very important to me. In this case everything was real – the sound of the bullets flying over people's heads, hitting into the cars and windows in the street, and the faces of the soldiers were so impressive that I couldn't use any other library sound to get the effect. And that was the style for all the film. Everything you see or hear in *The Revolution…* is real. And I think it was a good decision. Reality is impressive enough when you catch it with your camera.

Normally the *vérité* approach works to efface the role of the filmmaking in shooting and editing and constructing that 'reality' effect. However, there is a telling shot at the end of the film when Chávez, returning to Miraflores and sweeping down the palace corridors supported by a crowd, spots the filmmakers, turns directly to the camera and says: 'Show me the video of the night they took me away. I couldn't talk to you that night, but I knew we'd be back.' This significant and reflexive moment breaks the surface of the illusory self-effacement of the *vérité* mode.

OBJECTIVITY AND BALANCE

The perception of the documentary's form or style connects with arguments about the 'objectivity' of the film. At a formal and regulatory level factual television programmes are often discussed in terms of balance. This is an important formulation in media politics and those working in television stations have to carry a nuanced understanding of the concept. It was explained to me by Liz Forgan, who as Director of Factual Programmes had responsibility for fulfilling IBA (Independent Broadcasting Authority) guidelines at Channel 4. She outlined the parameters of political balance in terms of three levels of proximity. For the first category of programmes, in relation to distant international questions, there was a relaxed attitude to films with strong and enunciated points of view; although the television station should always be able to stand by all the individual programmes it has commissioned or transmitted, they were not covered by the criteria of balance. Political pressures get closer, she explained, within the category of general domestic political coverage which should achieve a rough balance across defined periods of time.[10] Individual programmes could indeed adopt tendentious perspectives, but the station's output should reflect all relevant points of view. However, closest to home, the third category was those programmes about heightened and controversial issues with a specific 'party political' dimension or those made within sight of an election. These demanded that each individual programme should be internally 'balanced'.[11] This last calibration might even have to be defended institutionally on the basis of precise, timed measurements of points of view when subject to political challenge. These relative levels of 'balance' are in television executives' minds as they judge the effects of contentious programmes.

Although Liz Forgan would not have described it this way herself, the above rules of balanced democratic argument are dispensed with when more is at stake –when the state is itself engaged in armed action. The particular *Panorama* programme that gave equal space to the pro- and anti-war positions as Margaret Thatcher's forces sailed towards a war in the Falkland Islands/Malvinas, the Thames Television programme *Death on the Rock* investigating the circumstances of the shooting of three IRA members by the British Special Air Service while on active service in Gibraltar on 2 March 1988,[12] and many other programmes that sailed too close to the armed conflict in Northern Ireland,[13] are examples that fall outside the normal parameters. There is a severe truncation of the space for critical commentary available in public media when the state is directly engaged in physical conflict. Such commentaries will encounter very formidable opposition if they try to challenge or undermine support for the state, even in a democratic society.

There are many other examples in relation to the conflict in Northern Ireland, the Falklands or Iraq; but one more esoteric example occurred in 1991 when, working for Channel 4, I had been to Hanoi several times to view feature films and programme a season called Vietnam Cinema. Some of the films dealt with the war (called 'the American War' by the Vietnamese) but most of them were concerned with other aspects of experience and were part of our attempt to bring a wider range of world cinema to British television screens. The eight-week season was scheduled for transmission when, at the last minute, Liz Forgan explained that it would have to be cancelled and delayed. The logic was explained in a fierce exchange of memos: the first Gulf War had just begun and she felt it was inappropriate for the Channel to be showing films which 'depict American soldiers being killed when real American soldiers are dying in the desert'. I tried to explain that the indigenous Vietnamese films were broadly humanist and even anti-war in approach and that they could not be described as anti-American. This was to no avail – it was a 'judgement of taste'; the season had to be delayed until the war was over.

Issues raised about the accuracy and balance of *The Revolution Will Not Be Televised* arose at a difficult time for at least one of the broadcasters. The BBC's ethos was under attack as a result of a Radio 4 news report about the government's justification for the Iraq War which had drawn the BBC into considerable political controversy. The Labour government claimed that the journalist involved had breached BBC guidelines on fair and objective reporting when he suggested that the government's Iraq dossier had been 'sexed up'.

However, concern with political integrity does not to lead to the disingenuous suggestion that we should shy away from committed documentary-making. All filmmaking has its *parti pris* – as the American filmmaker Emilio de Antonio once quipped, 'Only God is objective and he doesn't make documentaries'. There are obvious ethical dimensions to documentary-making and it is important that the process of choice and selectivity involved in constructing a film should not slip into intentionally inaccurate or evasive strategies. The audience should be able to maintain a basic level of trust in the veracity of the programme they are viewing – although this depends upon a consistent commitment, on the part of broadcasters and filmmakers, to accuracy and precision.

LOCAL MEDIA MISREPORTING

The structure of the media in Venezuela is dominated by a small number of commercial enterprises. Venevisión, the most watched network, is owned by Gustavo Cisneros, a Cuban-American mogul, dubbed 'joint-venture king' by the *New York Post*. The Cisneros Group has partnered many US brands – including AOL, Coca-Cola, Pizza Hut and Playboy – becoming a gatekeeper to the Latin American market. He asserted in 1999 that 'Latin America is now fully committed to free trade and fully committed to globalisation … as a continent it has made a choice' (quoted in Klein 2003).

The private television stations' pre-coup campaign against Chávez is detailed in *The Revolution Will Not Be Televised*. Their weak public service tradition, low journalistic standards and aggressive antagonism to the regime are carried into the coup attempt itself, with a news blackout. 'We [the coup organisers] had a deadly weapon: the media', as Vice-Admiral Victor Ramírez Pérez put it, speaking on Venevisión on 11 April. Andres Izarra, who trained in journalism abroad and became news director for RCTV, says he received clear instruction: 'No information on Chávez, his followers, his ministers and all others that could be related to him' (quoted in Klein 2003). When Chávez finally returned to Miraflores palace on one of the most important days in recent Venezuelan history, the station broadcast the feature film *Pretty Woman* (Garry Marshall, 1990). 'We had a reporter in Miraflores and knew it had been retaken by the Chávistas … [but] the information blackout stood. That's when I decided to leave' (quoted in Klein 2003). Izarra was appointed Washington Press Attaché and then Minister of Information in Chávez's subsequent government, and led the campaign against media destabilisation.[14]

After the coup, the private stations continued their aggressive anti-Chávez campaign. For example, Venevisión transmitted two panel discussion programmes on 3 and 10 October 2003 which disparaged and denounced *The Revolution Will Not Be Televised*. Chávez decided to tackle the television situation in earnest – 'Don't be surprised if we start shutting down TV stations' – raising the question of whether or not attempts to regulate the media are necessarily an attack on press freedom. The old paradigm in which all journalists want to tell the truth and all threats come from nasty politicians emanates from the myth of the role of the reporter in many fictional representations and is rarely sustainable in practice. Izarra asserted (in Klein 2003) that, as a result of the commercial media's campaign to oust the elected government, the four private television stations have effectively forfeited their right to broadcast: 'I think their licences should be revoked.' In

March 2005, legislation was announced which would subject Venezuelan radio and television to 'social responsibility' and invoke penalties of up to five years in prison for 'spreading false information' or 'inciting hatred'. After admitting the scale of the problem of an implacably hostile media, Phil Gunson, the *Economist's* correspondent, asserted that 'the government's cure for media bias is worse than the disease' (2005: n. p.) and José Miguel Vivano of Human Rights Watch in New York commented that 'imposing a straitjacket on the media is not the way to promote democracy' (quoted in Gunson 2005: n. p.).

The media community in Venezuela has had its own crisis of confidence: 'The common attitude has been that we can leave aside ethics and the rules of journalism,' explained Laura Weffer, a political reporter for *El Nacional* (quoted in Dinges 2005). Concerned reporters formed a group called *Los del Medio* ('those in the middle'). In the current polarised climate they were immediately characterised both as closet Chávistas by sceptical colleagues and described by government supporters as *Los del Miedo* ('those who are afraid') (see Dinges 2005).

There have been long explorations and debates in democracies about the statutory and non-statutory regulation of the press. They often spring from the unexceptional proposition that the media should be required to provide a consistent and conscientious service free from deliberate distortion or misreporting. Mass communication in our society is remote and unresponsive; there is a lack of accuracy, access and accountability for both the public service and private media. However, even if this principle is clear and can be agreed to, the implications of enforcement are characterised by reference to the dangers of state control. There have been few attempts to encourage popular participation or to devise any form of democratic control. Most politicians are concerned about the press and media attitudes at some point and then become immune to press hostility and inaccuracy and find ways to live with the vagaries of a commercialised, irregular press. 'It would be like a sailor complaining about the sea,' as the British politician Enoch Powell once remarked.

Rather than attempting to ban the commercial television stations or revoke their licences at that point, in July 2005 the government proposed to outflank them with other media. Andres Izarra launched a new pan-continental satellite television station, Telesur. Describing itself as an antidote to Western-controlled media hegemony and cultural imperialism, it is backed by the governments of Argentina, Cuba, Uruguay and Brazil and it screens documentaries by new filmmakers, and independent films dubbed 'Nojolivud' ('No Hollywood'). The station is committed to perspectives from Latin American countries ignored within those countries and by the international media. The Qatar-based television station Al Jazeera showed that inhabitants of the Arab world were enthusiastic for an indigenous perspective on conflicts in the Middle East. The driving force behind Telesur has been President Chávez; Venezuela has contributed 70 per cent of the station's $10m budget and owns 51 per cent of the company.

'Alternative' media may offer a challenge to dominant views, but first they have to market themselves to achieve a wide audience, and that is to enter an aggressively competitive sphere where commercial forces have advantage. While television and newspapers are significant factors in the determination of people's view of the world, the power of these channels is not absolute. There are other contexts – the experience and discussions of everyday life for instance – that feed into understandings. It can be argued that popular support for Chávez in Venezuela results less from the rather stolid programming of the government channel and more from 'word of mouth' popular discourse outside the media's domain.

INTERNATIONAL MISREPORTAGE

Concern about the role of the media should not only focus on the concerted activities of the Venezuelan media; international reporting of the actual coup attempt was significantly askew.

For example, to take a substantial British newspaper with a perceived liberal or progressive orientation, on 12 April 2002 *The Guardian*[15] ran a report under the by-line 'staff and agencies', entitled 'Venezuelan President Resigns after Coup'. It stated unequivocally that 'massive civilian demonstrations ... ended in government troops firing on protesters ... National Guard troops and pro-Chávez gunmen then opened fire on 150,000 anti-government protesters with bullets and tear gas' (Anon. 2002). This was followed a day later – the Saturday – by the report 'Ousted Chávez Detained by Army' (with a sub-heading: 'Venezuelan Military may Charge Former President over Bloodbath at Demonstration') under the by-line 'Alex Bellos, the *Guardian*'s South America Correspondent'. The story contained the unhesitating pronouncement that 'pro-Chávez snipers had killed at least 13 people', followed by the incriminating statement that 'witnesses saw rooftop snipers and Chávez supporters fire at the protesters and at ambulance crews trying to aid the wounded' (2002). The report included the background assertion: 'His popularity [had] plummeted as he antagonised almost every sector of society and failed to improve the lot of the poor' (ibid.). Alex Bellos then based himself in Rio de Janeiro to write about football and Samba. Asked about the reports, he explained: 'From what I remember I basically rewrote the international wires – I was never there during the coup.'[16] Rewriting the 'wires' (information from Associated Press and Reuters) led to the *Guardian*'s reports of the *coup d'état* reproducing the uncorroborated claims of the Chávez opposition that had been disseminated that weekend. The significant difference between the first and second reports was that the first appeared to have emanated from 'staff and agencies' and the second under the designation of an individual carrying the professional imprimatur of the 'South America Correspondent'. This carries the wholly fallacious implication of a story from someone close to the events, if not an actual eyewitness report. Actually, Alex Bellos' job title and geographical location can be construed as misleading – 'rewriting the wires' could just as well have taken place in Berlin, Birmingham or Beijing.

On 12 April the BBC one o'clock television news ran a two-minute item cut in London from agency footage. Under the banner headline 'Venezuela Crisis' the presenter introduced the report with the following phrase: 'It is thought that Hugo Chávez chose to step down after armed forces withdrew their support for him.' BBC reporter George Eykyn provides a voiceover for the agency pictures that have been assembled into the short item: 'The beginning of the end for President Chávez. Up to half a million opposition supporters marching on his palace yesterday were tear gassed by troops and then shot at from the rooftops by gunmen loyal to Chávez.' This last pivotal phrase is spoken over the shot of the 'shooters on the bridge' and delivered with the confidence of 'Knowledge' and 'Truth' a middle-class English accent carries. The commentary has the pattern of the strange over-emphasis on arbitrary words in each sentence that often exemplifies tele-prompt readers trying to give an effect of meaning to the passing phrases they are enunciating. The short report on the Caracas coup was followed by an item on new tax breaks to tackle obesity in the US.

The BBC archive information sheet summarises the piece and logs the individual shots used together with their sources:

> The former Venezuelan President Hugo CHÁVEZ is being held at an army barracks in Caracas after being forced to resign by the country's military. (C) APTN-Protests, Tear Gas, Gun Men Shooting, President, Protest for strike, Tanks by Palace, Army Commander speaking not given, Chávez in crowd/Iraqi TV Via Agency – Chávez with Saddam/REUTERS – Night Shots CARACAS: Has huge anti-Hugo Chávez demonstration along road twds Presidential Palace, tear gas released; Has people making way as casualty is carried along amongst them; MS Pro-Chávez gunmen lying down on roof, firing at unseen demonstrators; MS man lying on ground after being shot, people milling around; MS President Hugo CHÁVEZ, wearing red beret, speaking into microphone; Var s striking oil workers clapping & standing behind barriers; Var s Venezuelan troops force open gates & walk into ground of oil company past striking oil workers. EX LIB: WSN212/00/8: Var s CHÁVEZ surrounded by supporters after winning the election. WSN225/00/5: BAGHDAD: MS CHÁVEZ meeting Iraqi President Saddam HUSSEIN. END EX LIB.

The BBC's deployment of the same medium shot of 'Pro-Chávez gun-men lying down on roof [sic], firing at unseen demonstrators' exemplifies the way in which the misinterpreted image of the 'shooters on the bridge' was used immediately and internationally to explain the coup.

The *Observer*'s Greg Palast asserts that the US State Department was active in misinforming American journalists about the process of the coup and it is astonishing to discover the way in which a pervasive image-system crosses the globe, reiterating authorised narratives which disclose events deceptively and depict the world with a specious consistency.

There was some increase in international attention to Venezuela after the coup, driven by greater recognition of the drama of the contention in

that part of the continent – 'Chávez has had his Bay of Pigs' as the English historian Eric Hobsbawn put it.[17] The press may have been somewhat
chastened by the surprise of the coup and its reversal, but the underlying
problem continues because 'few political reporters are interested in what
is going on in Venezuela, only the *Financial Times* and the *Economist* have
stringers in Caracas and both are dramatically hostile to Chávez', as Richard
Gott asserts.[18]

CONTEXT – INDEPENDENTS AT HOME AND ABROAD

Part of the critique of *The Revolution Will Not Be Televised* articulated by Venezuelan filmmakers based in that country and abroad is the fact that it was
made by outsiders. Maybe there is a particular resentment, an understandable basis for this sense of exclusion and perhaps a feeling of disenfranchise-
ment by the international (that is, Western) media. The inaccuracy of many
depictions by external filmmakers is often a cause of dissatisfaction. Michael Grade, when launching the Third World magazine programme *South*
for Channel 4 in 1991, quipped succinctly, 'most British television research
about the Third World takes place elsewhere – in Terminal 3 of Heathrow
Airport'. The developing world is rarely high on news agendas in the North
and when coverage occurs, it is often as a result of a dramatic conflict which
attracts a sudden short-term flurry of 'parachute journalists' and news crews.
To add salt to the wounds of indigenous filmmakers, the foreign reporters
and current affairs producers who fly in to Third World countries often use
local independents to facilitate the production of reports which are then
edited and controlled from their distant metropolitan centres.

The specific context of a home-grown independent sector with inadequate space for 'self-expression', which is used to being mediated by news
reports from elsewhere, may have informed some of the critique of a film
made by Irish independents. There is no specific evidence that the filmmakers' cultural/national distance from its subject affected the documentary,
but it raises the wider issue of what is at stake when filmmakers from outside communities that are experiencing major historical shifts are involved
in their representation. It is ironic that, in this case, the film was being made
by a three-person independent outfit from a small European country, it-

self with a relatively fragile and underdeveloped independent production sector. If the Northern media habitually included more direct speech from Southern filmmakers, then the compatible, complementary nature of documentaries from different places and perspectives might have constituted a healthier context of reception for Bartley and Ó Briain's film.

ASYMMETRICAL EXPECTATIONS

Channel 4's daily Duty Log made strange reading for most of the ten years I worked at the station. It noted the views of those who telephoned the station directly to complain or enquire and took viewer responses through to a programme called *Right to Reply*, (which was nicknamed the 'Right's Right to Reply' inside the channel, since indeed the bulk of political criticism came from the Right). There is no symmetry or equivalence in how elements of the Left respond to a programme which overturns or disregards its values, and how the Right responds to a programme it dislikes. The Left's antagonistic relationship with the media in general is predicated on the implicit assumption that television is part of the 'establishment' and at some level cannot be expected to be fair to, let alone be sympathetic to, radical, critical views. While the Right shares a suspicion that 'they are not on our side',[19] that there may be all too many liberal, 'pinko' journalists and programme-makers who have 'infiltrated' the media, it takes much more active and outraged offence in reaction to any transgression of its point of view.[20] At some level there is a different sense of relationship, of psychological ownership even – 'it's *our* television after all' – for some sections of the social formation.

If these asymmetrical expectations exist in relation to the European media, it is clearly more so in Venezuela where the attitudes of the ensemble of private television stations encourage aggressively Manichean and pejorative views of Chávez. The recent barrage of hostility was preceded by early pre-emptive attempts to characterise Chávez as ultra-nationalistic and militaristic, 'the Venezuelan *caras pintada*',[21] in the 1990s. His first trip to Cuba in December 1994 was greeted with extremely negative publicity and described by some of the Venezuelan press as confirming 'the axis of evil'. There has been a long and consistent reinforcement of the Venezuelan middle-classes' expectations of the media and of convictions that Chávez was unsupportable and his regime disastrous.

Disinclination to take Chávez seriously was also revealed in other quarters – the early restoration of his power certainly caught a British government minister offguard. On Saturday 13 April Denis MacShane, Labour MP for Rotherham and Minister for Latin America at the Foreign Office, and a former journalist himself, published an article in the *Times*. Under the headline 'I saw the calm, rational Chávez turn into a ranting, populist demagogue', he wrote that he had met the President the week before: 'He was dressed in a red paratrooper's beret and rugby shirt and waved his arms up and down like Mussolini – an odd, disturbing spectacle' (2002). Of course the Minister was forced to retract and 'welcome his return to office' two days later; although one can still discern an underlying desire for regime change: 'Last week's coup has failed. Any change of government should come about by democratic means' (quoted in White 2002). Ill-judged intervention and abrupt *volte-face* revealed much more than ineptitude – it is another manifestation of New Labour's extreme centrist politics and anachronistic imperial patronage: 'Venezuela now needs to find its way to a democratic and inclusive governance in which social justice combines with economic modernisation. Britain will be there to help' (White 2002).

DIALECTICAL DETERMINATIONS

This analysis of *The Revolution Will Not Be Televised* strays into politics and history only in so far as it informs the life of the film. But in the arcane groves of philosophical and academic debate much attention has been paid to the relationship between the economic base of a society and its political superstructure. Karl Marx raised the question of the degree of determination economics might have on political formations and cultural discourses 150 years ago. At this stage of the unresolved debate the issue remains contradictory and attenuated, but the question has had its effects in all facets of politics, thought and culture. In 'What is to be Done?', a filmmaking manifesto issued by Jean-Luc Godard, Jean-Pierre Gorin and the Dziga Vertov Group, it is formulated simply as: 'The social existence of men determines their thought' (1970: point 8). In its simplest terms, Marx's approach proposed that underlying material disparities between different groups in society were the main factors in generating political change: 'Life is not determined by consciousness, but consciousness by life' (1845). However, even if it can be agreed that economic differences are generally a factor in social movement, they are often mixed in an ensemble of elements or are over-determined.

There is plenty of evidence of social and economic disparity in Venezuela, a country where the great majority of the population is permanently poor and hungry. While the top 10 per cent of the population of 23 million receives half the national income, 40 per cent, according to an estimate of 1995, live in 'critical poverty'. An estimated 65 per cent, according to the figures for 1996, earned the minimum wage or less. Social inequalities may be more apparent as real purchasing power declined by 35 per cent between 1989 and 1995.[22]

The orientation and policies of the Chávez regime may have posed a direct challenge to the material position and access to power of the upper-middle-classes in Venezuela, a stark threat to that group's lifestyle, power and influence;[23] it should therefore not be a shock that they embarked on a strong, unequivocal response to this challenge. The more complex question is the extent to which Chávez's policies actually constitute an objective threat to the interests of the wider middle classes; while his rhetoric is revolutionary, his reforms have been moderate and social democratic. He criticises the effects of the application of 'savage neo-liberalism' which has done so much harm to the poorer peoples of Venezuela and Latin America in the past twenty years, but he is no state socialist; the private sector is alive and well. His land reform is aimed chiefly at unproductive land and provides for compensation (see Gott 2005c: 157–65). As Donnacha Ó Briain puts it:

> Chávez is essentially a Keynesian reformist, he's not about revolutionary appropriation of property. Of course the middle classes indeed did act *as if* he was about to steal the leather sofa from under their arses – but that is another thing altogether. The real threat Chávez posed was to the super-rich oligarchy which arguably has very few mutual class interests with the middle class, but has managed to turn them into allies.

The formation of an intransigent, wider middle-class opposition, based more on ideology and racial antipathy than on material loss, is a key problem faced by Chávez's social project. Unlike the Cuban revolution decades earlier, initial middle-class support for Chávez evaporated early on.[24] Interestingly, during her brief sojourn in Caracas, bringing a Cuban perspective to Chávez's predicament, Aleida Guevara conducted several interviews in the Venezuelan press and on television suggesting that he had been 'too soft on opponents' such as those who executed the failed *coup d'état* in 2002 (2005: 141, fn 35).

Chávez's achievement has been to channel increased oil revenues into a fresh range of social projects which bring health and education into neglected shantytowns. This redeployment of oil revenues may have had some effect on the material interests of the bourgeoisie as they had been used to high levels of state funding in the cultural industries. Chávez sees the revenues from the state oil company Petroleos de Venezuela (nationalized in 1975) as a one-off opportunity to educate a new generation of Venezuelans who have never had access to adequate resources. The aspiration is the emergence of a fresh and inclusive polity – educated and healthy – that will make its own decisions about the future direction of society.

POLITICAL POWER GROWS OUT OF THE BARREL OF A GUN

At a risk of stating the obvious, the dynamic this film records is well outside the minor oscillations of the 'normative' political activities and discourses of most democracies in periods of relative calm. The phenomena that the film has caused indicate what is at stake: the balances of prosperity and power in one country, the politics of an entire region and indeed continent. As Graham Greene wrote, 'in these countries [Central and Latin America] politics have seldom meant a mere alternation between rival electoral parties but have been a matter of life and death' (1984: 12).

Following the material motivations of contending classes, the decisive role of the armed forces in the resolution of the conflict is clear; *The Revolution Will Not Be Televised* records the determined move made by the palace guard on the afternoon of 13 April – when they seized the building of Miraflores as the simulacrum of power – but this is representative of the larger-scale shifts in military/political alliance. The film clearly indicates that popular mobilisation was also a key factor in the resolution of the conflict. The relative roles of popular support and shifts within the armed forces are difficult to gauge because the two factors go hand in hand. Colonel Baduel in Valencia is a case in point; he continued to support Chávez during the coup, helped by the noisy presence of Chávistas arriving outside the barracks.

The role of the armed forces sits uncomfortably with a Left used to other alignments. The Left critique of the regime points out that a radical military regime is still a military regime and there must be an understandable wariness of armed forces having such a high degree of influence and control in civil society. Douglas Bravo, who was a guerrilla leader in Falcón in the 1960s, takes the view that 'Chávez did not want civilians to participate as a concrete force. He wanted civil society to applaud but not to participate, which is something quite different' (quoted in Gott 2000: 63). Chávez puts it another way: 'The idea is to return the military to their basic social function, so that both as citizens and as an institution, they can be incorporated into the democratic development projects of the country' (quoted in Gott 2000: 225). There are specific reasons for this approach. Chávez's lack of support in the civil service infrastructure meant that he fell back on the military resources he knew so well.

There will also be inevitable criticisms from the Left regarding the inadequate speed and degree of social change. In an earlier era, such arguments were rebutted by Omar Torrijos, President of Panama: 'My idea of the ultra-left is this: they make a cowardly escape by planning a future revolution which never becomes a reality … There is no reason to pay a high price for social change. If it is not necessary, why do it?' (quoted in Greene 1984: 135).

One of the central ironies of this moment in Venezuelan history is that the *coup d'état* attempted in 2002 was perpetrated on an ex-coup plotter. This irony was invoked in debates about the film at the rough cut stage. It seemed important to both filmmakers and funders that this background be inserted in voice-over, perhaps to recognise the circularity of 'the biter bit'. This was also a way of avoiding that historical weakness of the Left – to suppress inconvenient detail, difficult and contradictory information – in an insistence on recording the actual complexity of the world. The original coup plotter of 1992 was in power as a result of due electoral process: that democratic mandate had been ratified eight times, the most recent examples being the recall referendum on 18 August 2004, when Chávez achieved 58 per cent of the vote in an internationally monitored poll[25] and the Presidential election of December 2006 when he achieved 63 per cent.[26]

AMBIGUOUS ASSESSMENTS

In 2000, Colombian novelist Gabriel García Márquez wrote an article entitled 'The Enigma of the Two Chávezes, Deliberate Ambiguity Breeding Doubts and Hopes'. Márquez sketched a portrait, ending his equivocal impression of Hugo Chávez with the phrase that he had 'gladly travelled and talked with two contrary men. One a self-styled visionary, whom inveterate luck has offered the opportunity to save his country. And the other, a conjurer who could pass into history as just another despot' (2000). Márquez invokes the dangerous legacy of the 'caudillo' figure in Hispanic politics. The apprehension of the anti-Chávista opposition is that not only does it not support the specific egalitarian policies of the regime (redistribution of land and oil revenues, community infrastructure and development) in the immediate future, but it might find that the imposition of his leadership will continue on a more permanent basis. Certainly Chávez had adeptly turned the moments of greatest threat into opportunities: the coup attempt enabled him to purge the armed forces of disloyal officers and the PVDSA management strike allowed him to reduce overmanning and consolidate power at all levels of the national oil company. Even television evangelist Pat Robertson's extraordinary public call for the United States to assassinate the elected President of Venezuela,[27] along with the State Department's recalcitrant response, played into his hands (see Guillermoprieto 2005b). Could belief in the moral necessity of the project draw Chávez and his supporters towards that threshold where the end justifies the means? There are too many examples where, as Jacqueline Rose says, 'ideals are a licence to kill' (in Mackenzie 2003).

Although complex argumentation around the political assessment of Hugo Chávez inevitably continues – and there is no reason to suggest that this will diminish in the foreseeable future – Márquez's poised hesitation between two such polar interpretations seems less tenable seven years after his election. Richard Gott was unambiguous in his summation when he wrote in 2005: 'the chrysalis of the Venezuelan revolution led by Chávez, often attacked and derided as the incoherent vision of an authoritarian leader, has finally emerged as a resplendent butterfly whose image and example will radiate for decades to come' (2005a).

As always, there is an important distinction between criticism that seeks to further the process of radical change and that which seeks to reverse it. Although many broadly sympathetic commentators might go on to point to limitations in the Chávez project or problems with his style of leadership, it is clear that it has reopened a radical social agenda for Latin America. If there are shortcomings, surely their critique can lead to better and more consistent approaches to attaining the same ends.

From some points of view, Chávez represents a most unprecedented combination of democratic means and significant structural change. Certainly it can be argued that (alongside Salvador Allende and Alexander Dubcek), perhaps Hugo Chávez's version of 'twenty-first century socialism' poses greater contradictions for the dominant ideologies of the West and signifies a more proximate threat than other versions of radical politics, because at its core is a democratic vision.

COMMITMENT

Eppur si muove.

Nevertheless it moves.

The final irony of the firestorm that broke over the film entitled *The Revolution Will Not Be Televised* arises precisely from the fact that it *was* televised. It was transmitted under the auspices of the BBC and other stations in Europe and then in Venezuela, its own political domain. Although it countered many aspects of normal news and current affairs depictions of the Third World in the northern hemisphere, the most forceful reaction was from Venezuela, where it was seen by those opposed to Hugo Chávez as dangerous and as a partial representation of their recent political history.

The arguments around the film raise complex issues of objectivity and commitment for filmmakers everywhere. Jean-Luc Godard and Jean-Pierre Gorin, in Point 22 of 'What is to be Done?', proposed the injunction 'not to fabricate over-complete images of the world in the name of relative truth' (1970). With this, they pointed to the dialectics involved in holding an equilibrium between adequate complexity and lucidity in a complicated world, and the desire to make films which proposed radical interpretations of that reality.

Lucia Astier, a Venezuelan filmmaker and editor who was critical of *The Revolution Will Not Be Televised*, suggests that Kim Bartley and Donnacha Ó Briain had to rearrange their material because it 'would lack that assured gripping quality that comes from absolute moral certainty'.[1] She ignores, however, an important delineation in the meanings of the film: while it might find moral certainty in its exposition that an attempt to overthrow a democratically elected government by orchestrated violence is unequivocally wrong, that does not necessarily lead to unequivocal support for all aspects of the regime that the coup was attempting to topple. Every individual filmmaker has to calibrate the issues, make political assertion more accurate, moral argument more honest and their films clearer and more effective for audiences. There are no pre-emptive positions in documentary-making or in politics and we cannot think on behalf of others. Filmmakers have to develop and strengthen the register of innovative creative forms adequate to their political tasks. As Lindsay Anderson suggested in an elegant and dialectical formulation shortly after making the 1968 feature film *If...*: 'The older you grow, the more you are conscious of and believe in and have to accept the ambiguities of existence . . . and you know that in every truth the opposite is also true. The very important thing is to perceive *that* truth, and yet hold the opposite of *that* truth, which is that there *is* a truth' (quoted in Sussex 1969: 75).

The Italian writer Franco Solinas, talking in a different context about *The Battle of Algiers* (a feature film he wrote with Gillo Pontecorvo in 1965), said that 'movies have an accessory and not a decisive usefulness in the various events and elements that contribute to the transformation of society. It is naïve to believe that you can start a revolution with a movie and even more naïve to theorise about doing so. Political films are useful, on the one hand, if they contain a correct analysis of reality, and on the other, if they are made in such a way to have that analysis reach the largest possible audience.'[2] Indeed the achievement of the makers of a seminal film like *The Battle of Algiers* is their ability to depict a dramatic and historic conflict – the struggle between French forces and the Algerian National Liberation Front – with adequate complexity and honesty in the face of the moral contradictions of political violence, while leaving the spectator in no doubt about the film's committed view of the historical process or the justice of the anti-colonial cause.[3]

By depicting the political initiative represented by Chávez and the forms of response to his movement, *The Revolution Will Not Be Televised* implicitly asks whether or not radical social change is possible and, if so, on what terms. It also asks what forms progressive representations of such a process of change might take – it confronts the formidable task of retaining a radical aspiration, remaining lucid and yet not allowing commitment to eliminate complexity and contradiction. If one accepts political responsibility for one's own utterances, one has to assess everything that one says publicly and the effects it will have in a concrete historical context.[4]

Understandably, in certain circumstances, this may lead to different forms of self-censorship and inhibition. Others may exploit aspects of a carefully nuanced critique in order to undermine a figure or a movement that the author broadly supports. But such hesitations and self-restraints cannot, in the end, deflect from honest depiction of messy and overdetermined political processes; reflexive self-criticism is a healthy and indeed crucial component of those processes.

I witnessed an unexpected interaction at a press conference in London in May 2006 when a correspondent for the BBC's Spanish service asked Chávez 'Are you like Bush – demanding that we must be for you or against you?' Chávez's initial retort was fiery: 'Don't compare me with Bush – he is a criminal, a genocidal maniac.' But, after a pause, he replied with a more relativist response: 'Nobody has the absolute truth – it is only fundamentalists that claim to have it.'[5]

AFTERWORD

Obscuris vera involvens.
The truth being enveloped by obscure things.

In the years since *The Revolution Will Not Be Televised* was completed, a consistent belligerent effort to undermine the Chávez regime has taken place both in Venezuela and internationally.[1] Immediate and continuous antagonism from the indigenous opposition is accompanied by long-term reactive pressure from the United States against a government that it has decided to discredit and destroy. Perhaps it would be naïve to expect less. Venezuela offers an explicit challenge to the hegemony, whether it is the irreverence of Chávez's reference to the devil ('I smell the whiff of sulphur') as he followed George Bush at the podium in the United Nations assembly, or the offer of cheap heating oil to the North American poor. Hugo Chávez offers direct defiance to the dominant world power. Though preoccupied with other, more violent, skirmishes in the Middle East, the United States perceives correctly that its sphere of influence on the continent of Latin America could be jeopardised with several regimes now sharing politics explicitly critical of its role in the region and several others indicating more independent alignments.

This is a relevant time for the image of Chávez's twenty-first century socialism to play a more significant role in global politics.[2] There has been a sense that, since the fall of the Berlin wall, there has been reduced pressure on Western economies for a compromised balance of power between all sections of the social formation. European postwar social structures were predicated on the new balance of power that emerged in the Cold War. For instance, the new deal that constituted the postwar settlement in Britain included a historic compromise in health and education, the welfare state. The spectre of socialism, whatever its long nightmares of authoritarian political repression, represented an alternative to late capitalist social arrangements.

At the point when the Eastern socialist regimes disintegrated, and it seemed like it was the end of a life-cycle for socialism ('that great fallen oak of political endeavour' (see Debray 2007: 5); there was a moment of unrestrained triumphalism exemplified by the short-lived assertion of 'the end of history'.[3] Nearly twenty years since the end of socialism in Russia and Eastern Europe, Western regimes began to retrieve important components of previous compromises: the state sector was privatised and reduced rather than modernised and expanded; extensions of education and health were accompanied by incursions into free provision. These shifts to the centre (right) have been accompanied by a hollowing out of politics, with lower levels of popular interest and participation, the decay of involvement in political parties and smaller proportions of the population taking part in successive electoral processes in a depoliticised democracy (see Mair 2006).

At this historical moment Venezuelan visions and versions of social organisation are relevant, and although Chávez's approach is specific to its time and place, as with the legend of Simón Bolívar in eighteenth-century Paris it may have some effect in post-colonial Europe where belated recognition of proximate ecological crisis may necessitate rethinking social organisation and activity. In a new global context, the fragments of old Europe may consider novel alliances with the countries and continents of the developing world.

It is clear that substantial resources and direct efforts are being made to counter and contain what the US State Department explicitly sees as a 'strategic threat' to the region. In 2005, $6 million was allotted for its interventions (see Golinger 2006: 133). At this point evidence of US involvement in the coup remains fascinating, but circumstantial, such as the extraordinary incident days before the coup on 8 April 2002 where a US Marine officer David Cazares mistook Chávez loyalist General Roberto Gonzales Cardenas for coup-plotter General Nestor Gonzales Gonzales at a formal farewell reception for the Chinese military attaché in Caracas. Not realising that there were two General

Gonzaleses in the Venezuelan military High Command, he approached the wrong one (the name tag on a general's uniform only says the first last name). Apparently he said 'Why haven't you contacted the ships that we have on the coast and the submarine submerged in La Guaira? What has happened? Why has no one contacted me? What are you waiting for?' Puzzled by the questions, the wrong Gonzales merely took his business card and replied 'I'll find out' (see Wilpert 2007a). It is clear that many well-paid and highly skilled operatives are currently formenting a wide array of covert and unattributable activities. Philip Agee's revelations from a previous epoch in *Inside the Company: CIA Diary* (1975) established the scale and detail of North American intervention in the political processes of their Southern neighbours.[4]

The report of the office of the Inspector General of the US State Department, 'US Policy Toward Venezuela: November 2001–April 2002', written in reply to a formal question from Senator Dodd about involvement in the coup attempt and dated 3 May 2002, is a curious document. Like the State Department's Press Guide issued at the time,[5] it stretches the boundaries of 'credible denial'. Reiterating that 'The United States was absolutely not involved in the effort to remove Venezuelan President Chávez from power' it betrays a patronising and pompous tone: 'We are pleased that the hemisphere is engaged in supporting democracy in Venezuela.' Occasionally underlying and inappropriate manipulations are made visible. The imperative verbs in the following sentence reveal the attitudes of the hegemon at work in a sovereign country: 'On April 12 Ambassador Shapiro phoned Carmona and *told him* that any political transition process had to be constitutional and democratic and *urged him* not to dissolve the national assembly' (emphasis added). It should be noted, however, that American democratic frameworks at least facilitate a minimum process of accountability and enable a political representative to attempt to hold public service institutions to account for themselves.

A FAIRY TALE AT CHRISTMAS

A small but significant example of aggressive misinformation arose when, on 4 January 2006, the Los Angeles branch of the Simon Wiesenthal Center, a Jewish human rights organisation, issued a statement condemning

Chávez for anti-semitism in comments he had made in a speech on Christmas Eve. The exact quotation from his speech used in the statement was: 'The world has wealth for all, but some minorities, the descendants of the same people that crucified Christ, have taken over all the wealth of the world.'[6] This apparent 'reactionary and medieval rhetoric' was linked to the Iranian President Mahmoud Ahmedinejad who had 'denied the Holocaust' and was interpreted by the Wiesenthal Center as evidence of anti-semitism. These allegations began to be circulated immediately: *Libération* carried an article by Jean-Hébert Armengaud on 9 January called 'Le credo antisémite de Hugo Chávez' ('The anti-semitic beliefs of Hugo Chávez') and American papers reported the remarks widely and immediately. The way in which media agendas feed off themselves ensures that a high proportion of media reporting is derived from other media. Even Chávez sympathisers may have assumed that it was not inconceivable that a populist Christian socialist might have strayed into prejudice.

These criticisms, however, were generated by selective, deceptive editing of the original speech to allow a specific mischievous interpretation; the full paragraph from Chávez's original speech provides a different context leading to different meanings:

> The world has enough for everybody but it has turned out that a few minorities – the descendants of those who crucified Christ, the descendants of those who expelled Bolívar from here and also those who in a certain way crucified him in Santa Marta in Colombia – they took possession of the riches of the world, a minority took possession of the planet's gold, the silver, the minerals, the water, the good lands, the oil, and they have concentrated all the riches in the hands of a few; less than 10% of the world's population owns more than half of the riches of the world.[7]

The full quotation, with its inclusion of references to Simón Bolívar alongside Jesus Christ, clearly indicates that Chávez is referring to the rich rather than Jews; as an American Rabbi put it, 'no one accuses the Jews of fighting against Bolívar'.[8] Fred Pressner, President of the Confederation of Jewish Associations of Venezuela, speedily refuted the allegations and reprimanded the Simon Wiesenthal Center: 'You have interfered in the political status, in the security, and in the well-being of our community. You have acted on your own, without consulting us, on issues that you don't know or understand' (quoted in Perelman 2006). Chávez's perspective is clear in another speech he made on 5 December 2006, when, quoting extensively from the Sermon on the Mount, he asserts 'Christ was a radical rebel, a man of justice, that's the reason why he was crucified by the capitalists of his time, the imperialists' (Chávez 2007). Chávez spoke about the allegations in the National Assembly on 13 January 2007, refuting the charges and accused the Wiesenthal Center of 'following the instructions of the empire'.

Of course, even careful explanation that the allegations proved to be based on a partial quotation, used out of context, reaches only a fraction of the audience that received the original inaccurate version of the story. The black propaganda has already been effective in creating a loose penumbra of negative connotation around the perception of Chávez and his politics. *Post hoc* analysis does not retrieve the damage done and belated correction after the event, while welcome, has minimal effect. There are always reasons to be reluctant to accept a conspiratorial version of events speculatively or prematurely; but it is difficult not to believe that, like the 'shooters on the bridge', this is an example of deliberate and dangerous misinformation, that semi-autonomous branches of the US administration continue to devote resources and skills to this assiduous, insidious work.[9] From communist dictator and anti-semite and, more recently, from drug-runner and terrorist supporter, the work to build a negative connotative image which isolates and demonises Chávez is pervasive.

RCTV AND THE TELEVISION LANDSCAPE

The media itself became a focal issue for the opposition after Chávez signalled his intention to revoke RCTV's licence immediately after a strengthened electoral performance in December 2006. The decision not to renew this licence in May 2007 was proposed as part of a range of policies that would accelerate a revolutionary process and this particular issue was seized on by the opposition as a focus of particular contention to propagate its narrative of Venezuela's continuing slide into dictatorship.

RCTV's brand of melodramatic *telenovela* (Brazilian soap opera) programming and commercial entertainment had been combined with a pronounced political antagonism to the government. It was described as a 'white supremacist channel' by Richard Gott: 'Its staff and presenters, in a country largely of black and indigenous descent, were uniformly white, as were the protagonists of its soap operas and the advertisements it carried. It was "colonial" television' (2007). Chávez's government decided that RCTV's failure to respect the constitution or national law for Social Responsibility in Radio and Television was a basis for not renewing their broadcast licence. RCTV had a proactive role in the attempted coup supporting the short-lived President colloquially known as 'Pedro il breve' ('Pedro the brief'). Failing to report the resurgence of popular support after collusion in the coup, it was actively supportive of the subsequent PVDSA management strike. 'Europeans would never allow a channel on their televisions to incite violence, support a coup, or break with the constitutional order', said Alejandro Fleming (in Sánchez 2007), the Venezuelan ambassador to the European Union.

The non-renewal of RCTV's licence raises interesting questions for debates about media regulation elsewhere as well. There are many implications of the decision that should be seen in relation to the regulation of public service and commercial broadcasting in the United States and in Europe (see Goumbri 2007). It is relevant to a renewal of previous debates about the statutory and non-statutory regulation of the press; these often circulate around the entirely reasonable proposition that the media should provide a consistent and conscientious service free from deliberate distortion or deception. Broadcast media in our society are remote and unresponsive; accuracy, access and accountability could be improved in both the public service and private media.

No effort is made in Western political structures to encourage popular participation or to devise any innovative form of more democratic control. This seems to arise from a situation in which, even if the principles are clear and unexceptional, the connotations of regulation are characterised by apprehensions about the dangers of state control. This enables those who wish to maintain the status quo to block the possibilities of change. The furore raised by the truncation of RCTV's signal predictably fell into these discourses of 'a free broadcaster vs the oppressive state' with little reference to the responsibilities of regulated media. The contending arguments do not always pause for precise definition of their terms. In the context of the overheated, oversimplified debates that rage around questions of contemporary politics in Venezuela, Gregory Wilpert's article, 'RCTV and Freedom of Speech in Venezuela', offers a calm, considered and complex view of the bases of many of the antagonistic generalisations: 'As with most questions about Venezuela there is almost complete disagreement' (2007a).

Arguments by the contending parties appear to miss one another as they are conducted on different grounds: Chávistas strengthen their arguments by pointing to the ownership of media outlets (95 per cent of all media outlets are privately owned); the opposition prefers to deploy statistics in relation to the number of stations and their potential to reach Venezuelans. Gregory Wilpert (ibid.) examines the share of viewers – what people actually watch. Before RCTV was replaced by TVes there was a choice of a spectrum where approximately 50–55 per cent of viewers watched programmes on opposition channels, 30–40 per cent on neutral or balanced stations and 20–25 per cent on pro-government broadcasters. After the replacement of RCTV the spectrum *may* now shift: opposition 15–20 per cent, neutral/balanced 40–50 per cent or more, pro-government 25–30 per cent. Wilpert notes that, with the closure of RCTV, the ratio of opposition orientated to government sympathetic television has moved from 2:1 to 1:1.7. 'Any opposition would be overjoyed by having such a ratio. In Venezuela, of course, where the opposition is used to having ruled the country for four decades, such a disadvantage is an intolerable encroachment on their "freedom of speech"' (ibid.).

Access to a wide range of international television continued after the changes: RCTV now joins the international and external stations available by cable, for those with appropriate and expensive equipment. Satellite offers access to the familiar signals of CNN and BBC. The new Pan-Latin American channel Telesur is now joined by Al Jazeera in an English-language version; these stations represent Southern perspectives that challenge the pervasive American and European Media.[10]

Venevisión, owned by media mogul Gustavo Cisneros, currently reaches 20–25 per cent of the population. Initially it had an aggressively antagonistic stance to Chávez, but in 2004, despite Cisneros' corporate and political proclivities, the station underwent a discernable shift to relatively neutral and balanced reporting in 2004, after that summer's recall referendum. One can speculate that business interests led to accommodation as the economic bottom line, as it is colloquially known, asserted itself. Also Televen (with the smaller viewership of 10–15 per cent of the population) became more balanced after the referendum in 2004. Globovisión (watched by perhaps 10 per cent of the audience) has continued to offer a consistently and fiercely anti-government point of view. The terminal decline of the previous parties, AD and COPEI, has led to the media taking the roles of centres of opposition to the government, effectively replacing the old parties. They are working to de-legitimate a political system that has consistently provided Chávez with a democratic mandate.

There are also specialist niche broadcasters generally watched by a small proportion of viewers: Vale TV, Meridiano, Puma, La Tele. Uncontentiously ANTV offers a televisual 'feed' from the National Assembly – although it may be democratically important to have this available – realistically it is rarely watched. Pro-Chávez alternatives include the educational station ViVe – a station run by Blanca Eekhout, who had worked with a Caracas community television station CATIA TV – and the government-controlled VTV/Channel 8. This was a dramatic focus in the struggle for media control during the coup and is currently viewed by approximately 15–20 per cent of the viewers. A state channel since the 1960s, it is occasionally characterised as 'Albanian TV' – it includes intelligent dialogue and chat shows, but an overall dull and lifeless tone is underlined by repetitive interstitials of public service announcements about what 'the Bolivarian government has achieved...' from hydro-electric projects in the provinces to pavement improvements in the capital. This provision of government information and communication is normal and legitimate, but it is antithetical to contemporary televisual modes; the worthy tone is a kiss of death to any notion of attractive contemporary television. These perspectives are, of course, culturally determined; but it cannot approach the eye-catching, alluring signal by which international television attracts its audience at this time. For example, my experience developing new forms of programming in the early 1980s, as part of early Channel 4, indicates that progressive politics should be accompanied by colour, music, energy, sexuality.

THE IMAGE SYSTEM

The coverage in the *Irish Times* on 29 May 2007 of the contention around RCTV provided a relevant example of how image and text interact in contemporary reportage. A short article by Brian Ellsworth 'in Caracas' summarises the contention with relative accuracy and balance: reporting that 'the opposition media has been widely accused of violating basic journalistic standards' and that Chávez was 'forging a one-party state' he quoted a poll indicating that 70 per cent of Venezuelans were opposed to RCTV's closure, but cited the loss of their favourite soap opera rather than concerns about freedom of expression. Alongside his short article the paper printed a close-up photograph of a young woman with a gag and a slogan over her mouth. It makes a dramatic image – issues of censorship are always a hot topic.

Both picture and article were distributed by the Reuters news agency. Niall Fitzgerald, Reuters' Chairman, explained that the original journalist

'A supporter of RCTV taking part in a protest march in Caracas at the weekend along with tens of thousands of other Venezuelans': original caption from the *Irish Times*, 29 May 2007 (Photograph: Christian Veron/Reuters)

may have selected several pictures to go out alongside his story.[11] After the story is chosen it would normally be the role of the sub-editor to find images to accompany selected stories. Paddy Smyth, the paper's Foreign Editor, indicated that as the stories are updated throughout the day a choice of pictures arrive separately, even from the same agencies. Each story may be accompanied by between four and eight photos, leading to a choice of literally hundreds of picures from agencies all over the world, everyday. 'We look for something entertaining that illustrates the story, not PR, politicians' poses or line-ups.'[12]

The *Irish Times* subscribes to two wire services: Reuters and PA. Given the economic constraints on deploying a wide range of foreign correspondents it is the agencies, alongside syndication services from other papers (the *Guardian*, the *Financial Times* and the *Los Angeles Times/Washington Post* in the case of the *Irish Times*) that are often the main source of foreign coverage. The relative timing of the electronic arrival of the reports that emanate from the disparate timezones around the globe is significant. Paddy Smyth talks of the 'good timing' of material from the *Los Angeles Times*, whose journalists are filing articles at the end of their day which is early morning in Europe. Reuters and PA both send the *Irish Times* about fifty stories an hour, updating old stories regularly as they move on. The copy may be edited for length but its overall meaning or balance should not be changed. Paddy Smyth suggests that most alterations to Reuters copy are for reasons of style: '"Caracas, Venezuela" becomes just "Caracas", and "leftists" becomes "left wingers"'.

The article by Brian Ellsworth republished in the *Irish Times* is not unreasonable, but it has minimal impact in relation to the power of the accompanying image. The photograph is memorable and conclusive – it 'says it all'. Like the captioned footage of 'the shooters on the bridge', issued on the day of the attempted *coup d'état* in April 2002, it may be assimilated at speed and provides a seemingly irrefutable meaning.[13]

Speculatively one may analyse the conjunction of image and text as an interesting interaction of the combination of motives that make up media practice. Contrasting 'ideology' as unconscious assimilated attitude and 'conspiracy' as deliberate, conscious action, we may understand that ideological components played a role in selecting and recording this particular picture. The demonstration was part of an organised, deliberate, political intervention. The story is newsworthy and Reuters' International News Editor, knowing it would be written about by their reporter, would probably have ensured the event should be 'covered' by a news photographer as well: a handsome young woman making a dramatic gesture – the gag across her mouth – provides a striking composition. This story and picture was offered internationally by an independent news agency, into a context where 'conspiratorial' activities have ensured that the dominant narrative is one of Chávez's supposed increasing authoritarianism.

Ideological motives then ensure it finds a prominent place in the inevitably selective coverage of foreign events in a broadsheet newspaper. A dramatic image of a pretty girl is likely to appeal to newspaper editors. Paddy Smyth describes the photo as 'irresistible – there can be no hesitation about using it' and Hugh Linehan, Features Editor on the same paper, echoes the sentiment: 'A photo like that triggers a Pavlovian response for newspaper editors all over the world.'[14] It would be ludicrous, as well as libellous, to suggest that the Foreign Editor of the *Irish Times* was somehow hand-in-glove with the Central Intelligence Agency and Paddy Smyth is quick to point out that 'if the demonstrator had been a Chávez supporter instead of an opponent, she would have had exactly the same chance of getting into the *Irish Times*; this may not be true of other papers.'[15] However, we are witnessing a sophisticated combination where planned interventions work with predictable assumptions in the 'professional' (as in automatic and unconscious) functioning of media systems. Clearly a wider and more rigorous analysis is needed to indicate the extent to which these examples form a consistent pattern.

One must be careful to delineate the different arguments deployed in critique of these systems. Unlike the use of the 'shooters on the bridge' footage during the attempted coup, it is not the case that this image can be challenged as somehow misinterpreted or false, but in a world where many things co-exist as 'true' we should be aware of the processes of selection and their implications. There are always so many possibilities for representation, so many people, places, events. The range of image possibilities within any given event is enormous. What do we choose and why? Substantial resources for skilled expertise in communications and marketing has been made available to the Venezuelan opposition. This leads to effective media manipulation at source and those smart enough to set up attractive photo opportunities are making themselves felt in the international perception of Chávez's actions.

The arguments for and against RCTV continuing to have a role as broadcaster in a democratic system are complex and standard media reporting does not reflect that complexity. It is possible that intentional nefarious intervention was involved in the deployment and distribution of this story that, allied with the assumptions used at the speed of habitual journalistic process, led to an oversimplified and arguably biased result. Whilst one can try to generate discussion within the media to focus on such problems, denunciation is, as always, insufficient. It is not sensible for anyone on the receiving end of 'black propaganda' to turn their back on the image system. There is no alternative but to work to shape and position strong imagery from opposing points of view.

MOVEMENT ON THE GROUND

In the country itself the Venezuelan government articulated a strong case for its decision not to renew the licence for RCTV and this was clearly understood and accepted by the majority of its supporters. The profusion of arguments in the local press and evidence of visual slogans on the streets of Venezuela indicated all the internal implications for debates in an extremely polarised society. The opposition had clearly decided to challenge this decision head on and did so with some vigour. Apart from demonstrations, students who demanded to put their views to the National Assembly were allowed to do so.

Outside Venezuela the government tried to explain its motives, even producing *Say the Truth!* a free DVD based on the *White Book on RCTV* which was widely distributed. It counters extracts of RCTV's programming and its unrelenting anti-government half-truths with a critique which includes ex-employees who describe the enforcement of a narrow political view within the organisation and moralistic condemnations of some of the titillating programming. These partial arguments should be seen as a contribution to a more complex debate that never takes place as points are exchanged from entrenched positions. In Britain a letter supporting the decision co-or-dinated by the Venezuela Information Centre, was published by the *Guard-ian* on 26 May 2007 with 24 signatories, including the present author: 'RCTV gave vital practical support to the overthrow of Venezuela's elected govern-ment in April 2002 in which at least 13 people were killed ... In Venezuela, as in Britain, TV stations must adhere to laws and regulations governing what they can broadcast.' There was a swift response from the Venezue-lan opposition signed by over forty people including Napoleón Bravo, the same anti-Chávez television commentator who hosted that 'extraordinary television moment' included in *The Revolution Will Not Be Televised*, which revealed the integral role of RCTV in the orchestration of the coup. His reply that 'we were repelled by the letter...' was published by the same paper on 7 June. It singled out Harold Pinter's support for denunciation: 'It is shameful to see a Nobel prize-winner supporting moves that further restrict freedom of speech in our country.'

POST-RCTV – THE POSSIBILITY OF INDEPENDENTS

The point at which RCTV's transmission ceased as its licence to terrestrial broadcast was not renewed, represented a moment of change which can be seen as a potential turning-point for the current development of the media in Venezuela. Post-RCTV, dynamic new elements are emerging in a fast-changing media terrain.

From midnight on Sunday, 27 May 2007 a new channel was launched; the regulatory authority CONATEL (Comision Nacional de Telecomunica-ciones República Bolivariana de Venezuela) allotted RCTV's share of the broadcast spectrum to TVes, literally 'you see yourself', a new public service broadcast station. Although it had set up and funded the new channel and appointed its chief executive, the government had indicated that it would support the independence of the TVes board's editorial autonomy. The new station began by developing plans for achieving a mixture of financial resources. Lil Rodrigues, an ex-music producer from the satellite channel Telesur, formulated the channel's approach by redefining and reviving a no-tion of public service television which would focus on culture and sport, promote diversity and remind all Venezuelans of their AfroVenezuelan heritage. TVes combines serious and informative programmes with lighter material such as imported Argentinian soaps. Structurally it is a publisher-broadcaster supplied by independent producers; this leads to an on-screen texture of diversity less easy to achieve within a traditional vertically-integrated broadcasting model.

It is significant that these dynamic media developments take place at the moment of a new political context – the formation of a new party, the PSUV (United Socialist Party of Venezuela). Invited to subscribe at hundreds of local centres, 5.5 million new members signed up over four weekends in June 2007. Chávez's foundational speech on 15 December 2006 had indicated awareness of 'Stalin's deviation' whereby the Bolshevik party 'lost its nature and ended up as an anti-democratic party... "All power to the Soviets" turned into "All power to the Party"' (2007: 33).

The PSUV is an entirely new political structure designed to connect to the participatory democracy that has played a role in the implementation of radical social policies during the last five years. Beneath the formal democratic mandate in elections and referenda, the less visible aspects of community politics are also significant. Noam Chomsky has written of Venezuelan people power: 'In principle it seems to be a very powerful and persuasive conception, but everything always depends on implementation. If there is really authentic popular participation in the decision-making that could be tremendously important. In fact that's essentially the traditional anarchist ideal' (quoted in Golinger 2007).

However, contradictory tendencies towards top-down management have also been manifest. This is not a simple question of an authoritarian approach from a leader schooled in military command and control structures at the top. The development and deployment of centralised power and authority in discourse can be taken up with physical effect. However, when overenthusiastic Chávista assembly members drafted a draconian penal code with penalties for 'insulting the Presidency' significantly Chávez refused to sign the legislation and referred it back.

Support for the growth of an independent television production sector is clearly a central policy with the potential to enact the pluralism written into the 1999 constitution. Article 6 describes Venezuela as 'democratic, participatory, elective, decentralised, alternative, responsible and pluralist'[16] and talks of realising the prospect of constructive democracy. 'Venezuela's Law on Social Responsibility in Television and Radio has ... also contributed to the diversification of the media landscape, in that it mandates that five hours of programming per day (between 5am and 11pm) for each station be produced by independent national producers, with no single producer contributing more than 20 per cent of this.'

Work produced by independent filmmakers has the potential to take a sharper focus, to be more imaginative aesthetically. It often enunciates a more intense polemic or vivid point of view. This is clearly connected with a process of production that is located outside large-scale institutions, allowing for a different sense of the texture of everyday life and a better configuration of its contradictions. The actual position of independent producers, and their specific mode of production in smaller units, can lead to different forms of collaboration with non-professionals. For groups and individuals that live and work as an integral part of their communities, the scale, structure and pace of their work can be more reflective and responsive. Independent filmmakers from their position in the world and the process of filmmaking that they are engaged in, are more able to articulate programmes with authenticity and complexity.

ACCESS

Television has an obligation to encompass diverse of points of view, give space to perceptions and perspectives from different communities of interest. One aspect of that pluralism should be the encouragement of a wider range of non-professionals, individuals and groups, to become involved in active participation in programme-making. Versions of 'access' programme-making was developed in the 1980s in British television with BBC's *Open Space* and *People to People* early in the broadcasting history of Channel 4. These small and early gestures towards democratic access to the media, which were understood by those involved to be small-scale incursions and inadequate at the time, have since been marginalised and abandoned in a shift where 'reality television' genres take prominence. The presence of direct community speech as part of a mixed menu of wide-ranging programmes is crucial for the health of national media.

In the spring of 2007 a striking slogan was sprayed in clear white capital letters on the office building in Caracas that houses CONATEL, the regulatory authority that refused to renew RCTV's licence, and designated TVes its succesor:

"NI PRIVADOS
NI DEL ESTADO
MEDIOS COMUNITARIOS
ANMCLA"
("Neither private, nor state – free community media, ANMCLA")

ANMCLA is a national association of free, community-based and alternative media that has begun to raise the profile and the argument for independent access to production in Venezuela.

There are more than thirty community television stations operating in the country as a whole; generally located in poor areas where support for Chávez is stronger, they are developing the role of alternative media. CATIA TV, based in metropolitan Caracas, formulated the slogan 'Don't watch television – make it'. It has been providing ordinary citizens with access to the media since 2000. A programmatic statement CATIA issued in 2006 talks of 'Television From, By and For the People' and refers to the decisive need for a 'revolution inside the revolution'; its transmissions are intended to make room for independent criticism of the national state. A space for internal debate can address problems, monitor shortfalls and insufficiencies in national policies and work to improve their implementation. Grass-roots democracy will generate healthy internal dissent and contention. The ANMCLA slogan seeks a third position between state and corporate interests in order to promote a process from which independent critique can emerge. Local television can provide a form of citizen empowerment and accountability that contributes to better governance.

Ávila television is a community-based inititative, set up in 2006 by the mayor of Caracas. It was originally planned as a mass communications school and organises a combination of media literacy and production training. Individuals undertake courses to analyse how the media work and also learn to make films and programmes themselves. These forms of training develop critical practitioners within a framework of understanding: 'We must learn to decolonialise the way we read, see and listen in order to develop a critical audience; we need a culture of analysis as an alternative to the cultural bombardment of the media.'[17]

Applicants for the two-year courses must carry recommendations from community groups – this aims to guarantee their relationship with a specific community. José Manuel Iglesias and Carlos Matute of Ávila talk of 'building a different narrative, not the moralism of government channels'. They are exploring a new model for journalism, in contrast to that developed by the urban, middle-aged, middle class. Their production utilises music videos and clips, alternating with views captured on the street. For instance, trailers intended to initiate 'Anti-Media Terrorism Squads' called BAM, ask people to participate and send in short films, made on DV, or made on mobile phones – reiterating 'there's no excuse'.

Their programmes have a social and political edge, articulated in youthful, urban and street-wise modes – critical politics are an assumption for the young who are averse to the straitlaced approaches of older generations. Forms of youthful politics, like Indymedia[18] internationally, take libertarian, anti-authoritarian, anti-institutional forms.[19] However, the scale and scope of interventions within a participatory democracy need to be defined in terms of their relations with larger power structures. In the historical example of the extensive series of documentaries Joris Ivens and Marceline Loridan made in China, *How Yukong Moved the Mountains* (1976), the documentaries revealed over twelve hours the lively and argumentative debates going on in school rooms and workplaces. The filmmakers' enthusiasm for what they were shown was not related to the authoritarian structures that rigidly contained such free discussions and controlled the social policy as a whole. In this case the films indicated the performance of open and productive argument and criticism locally, but effaced the lack of democratic input at any level beyond this. Filmmakers from outside are vulnerable to such transcultural misunderstandings and those who wished to undermine *The Revolution Will Not Be Televised* predictably accused the filmmakers of falling into the same trap.

The relation between the criticism and practice of Venezuelan politics is often complex both at home and abroad. 'Solidarity should not be uncritical', as Greg Wilpert put it at a 2006 conference on Venezuelan democracy in London.[20] 'Opposition criticism is no substitute for constructive criticism from those who support the revolutionary project' writes Steve Ellner in 'The Trial (and Errors) of Hugo Chávez' (2007). It is not as though Chávez or any other political leader can discover the key to the gate of the garden of Eden, or find the pass over the mountains to come upon the pre-formed paradise of Shangri La nestling in a hidden valley.[21] The Left should not settle into a symmetry with the Right, asserting Manichean dogmas with blind certitude; there must always be a way to hold onto the complexity of reality, to approach a contradictory truth with rational instruments.

Social change in Venezuela is a complex, messy human process combining advances with miscalculations and missed opportunities. It is exceptionally dynamic, especially seen from the context of our terrain of northern Europe, where politics is glacial and the only dynamic contention is whether there is room for one more politician or party to stand in the middle ground. Venezuela's versions of twenty-first-century socialism follow the specificities of its own culture and history;[22] its interactions and differences with the other countries on the same continent, let alone those on other continents, will be complicated and overdetermined.

MEDIA WAR

The Revolution Will Not Be Televised made its effect felt in 2003 and in the subsequent period the intensification and sophistication of the media conflict has grown. 'We are in the middle of a media war', said Willian Lara, Minister of Communication and Information in 2007. There is a wide understanding of the media as a central terrain of contention at this moment of radical social change.

Richard Gott's article 'The Battle over the Media is about Race as well as Class' (2007) outlines this historical process with lucidity; as the framework of opportunity and privilege are shifted and redesignated, a most forceful and emotionally energetic reaction takes place. He predicts that 'this symbolic battle will become ever more familiar in Latin America in the years ahead; rich against poor, white against brown and black, immigrant settlers against indigenous peoples, privileged minorities against the great mass of the population'. After describing the languorous blondes at RCTV's closing down party as 'pulchritudinous', an attribute for which middle-class Venezuelan women had become disproportionately renowned in Miss World contests over previous decades, Gott goes on to contrast these representations with 'the old, the ugly and the fat – a cross-section of most Venezuelans found on any bus or metro' (ibid.).

Any structuralist analysis looks for the underlying motives in relation to surface phenomena. It is easy to be distracted by the superficial – but do we get a different picture if we strive to look at the larger scale or longer term? Roland Barthes proposed that 'the goal of all structuralist activity, whether reflexive or poetic, is to reconstruct an "object" in such a way as to manifest thereby the rules of its functioning' (1972: 149). There are significant material and historical factors in the democratic shifts taking place. Even the critical commentator, Francis Fukuyama understands the economics of the movement underlying government support. In his 2006 article 'History's Against Him', he renegotiates the antagonism caused by material disparity in Venezuelan society; dismissing Chávez with the specious neologism 'postmodern dictatorship', Fukuyama allows that a redistributive compromise between groups would be necessary to restabilise the social order within the economic orthodoxy he approves of: 'Free trade alone is unlikely to satisfy the demands of the poor, and democratic politicians must offer realistic social policies to compete'.

Chávez's accession in 1998 was a nemesis and the legacy of decades of extreme and hierarchical difference is still a decisive factor in the contemporary dynamic of radical change. His actions, in confronting economic and social disparities, have exacerbated polarisation, but they address structural conditions that pre-existed his regime in Venezuela and, it has to be said, continue in many other countries in many parts of the globe. Philip Agee sees it as a wider historical process:

A movement started with the election of Hugo Chávez as President of Venezuela in 1998 that has become as important, in my opinion, as the wars for Latin American independence from Spain two hundred years ago led by Bolívar, San Martin, Sucre and others. It is a movement for national liberation that now includes Evo Morales, President of Bolivia, and

Rafael Correa, President of Ecuador and their supporting political parties – a movement primarily to end the power of the traditional oligarchies and United States influence. All three of these South American Presidents advocate, and are taking measures, like constitutional reform, to end capitalism and to build a socialism for the twenty-first century. It's a wave of change unthinkable only ten years ago, and I see no way the United States can stop it.[23]

In the West, the politics of revolution had been recast as an anachronistic concept by the end of the twentieth century, but while the pronounced disequilibrium of power and wealth continues, the impulse for radical change still evolves in different forms. Chávez's proclamations of 'twenty-first-century socialism' are examples of the possibilities of renewal. The basis of his moral conviction was made clear in a speech in London in May 2006: 'The strength of our commitment is irrevocable … capitalism was born here at the end of the eighteenth century in the industrial revolution, after feudalism. But from the beginning it was clear that capitalism was so cruel and inhumane, this gave birth to the seed that will destroy it …'.[24]

The motor of transformation is not the calcified tradition of received socialist dogma, but the continuing perceived disparities of material conditions. There will be constant renewed contention over wealth and power, representation and control, as emancipatory forces persist and metamorphose in a landscape of change.

NOTES

ACKNOWLEDGEMENTS

1   These two engagements are discussed in Rod Stoneman (1992; 2005).

INTRODUCTION

1   Proposal for documentary development finance for *Aló Presidente!* sent to The Irish Film Board on 29 January 2001.
2   This might have blocked the possible nomination for an Academy Award since the Academy rules for documentaries preclude a previous screening on television.
3   The new Bolivarian constitution, put in place by Chávez, included provision for the termination of a President's tenure on the basis of a recall referendum.
4   The film takes its title from Gil Scott-Heron's 1974 song. Heron sang of a better world where *'Green Acres*, [the] *Beverly Hillbillies*, and *Hooterville Junction* will no longer be so damn relevant'*, better in part because, as he suggests in the last line, rather than being on television, the 'revolution will be live'.

PRODUCTION

1   Cristopher Columbus was enthralled by the Venezuelan landscape in 1498 and referred to it as Tierra de Gracia (Land of Grace).
2   For an extended exposition of this project, see Stoneman (2005) and Rockett (2003).
3   TG4 is an Irish-language television station, established as a publisher broadcaster in 1996.
4   Lorraine Morgan, my personal assistant.
5   BSÉ funding round reference: 24 DOC D13.

6   *The New Yorker*, 10 September 2001.

7   Interview with Kim Bartley and Donnacha Ó Briain, 12 August 2004.

8   Starting in 1982, Channel 4 was Europe's first publisher broadcaster. For discussion of the executive production role see Lambert (1982: 153).

9   BSÉ funding round reference: 25 DOC P13.

10 This was a device we utilised several times when I was at Channel 4; however, such shotgun weddings rarely last as long-term marriages.

11 David Power to BSÉ 26 September 2001. BSÉ funding round reference: 26 DOC P13.

12 David Power, email to author, 5 December 2001.

13 Kevin Dawson, RTÉ Commissioning Editor, letter to David Power, 11 February 2002.

14 David Power, email to author, 2 November 2005.

15 BSÉ to Power Productions, 6 December 2001.

16 Interview with Michael McCaughan, 6 July 2004. All subsequent quotes in this volume are taken from this interview.

17 Chávez's reference to food production is an unwitting coincidence, with the same example standing for the economic predicament of a country with too high a level of foreign ownership and imports used in 'Sauce of Wonder' – referring to Worcestershire sauce – an article from the *Guardian* (11 December 1976), also appended to his book *In the Shadow of the Liberator* (see 2001: 233–35).

18 BSÉ proposal 26 DOC P13, 6.

19 Informal note of meeting with filmmakers on 25 September 2001, taken by the author.

20 Daniel Florence O'Leary's colourful life is sketched in O'Shaughnessy (2007).

21 The phrase 'caméra stylo' was originally formulated by Alexandre Astruc in 1948.

22 Kim Bartley, email to author, 1 June 2005. Other versions of these events suggest seven people were arrested in the Hotel Ausonia on 11 April; for example, see Wilpert (2007b).

23 Carlos Polanco, email to author, 21 December 2005.

24 *El Juego de Cuba* (*The Cuban Game*, Manuel Martín Cuenca, Spain, 1999).

25 Ángel Hernández Zoido, email to author, 3 November 2005. All subsequent quotes in this volume are taken from this email.

26 Interview with Donnacha Ó Briain, 12 August 2004.

27 Interview with Kim Bartley, 12 August 2004.

28 David Power, email, 10 September 2002.

29 Updated treatment for *Alo Presidente?*, 10 September 2002.

30 Interview with Kim Bartley, 12 August 2004.

31 Ibid.
32 Ibid.
33 Rod Stoneman, note of phone call to Nick Fraser, 21 October 2002.

RECEPTION

1 Donnacha Ó Briain speaks the commentary, representing the filmmakers' direct speech.
2 Supported by the Department of Independent Film and Video at Channel 4.
3 HBO eventually withdrew after lengthy negotiations to purchase the film for transmission in the United States, although the filmmakers' costs were covered by HBO.
4 All reviews accessed on www.metacritic.com during march 2006.
5 See http://www.metacritic.com (accessed 3 August 2008).
6 Marina Levitina, email to author, 20 November 2005.
7 In Caracas several years later on impulse I looked up W. Schalk in the telephone directory and, cognisant of how much our recent preoccupations had intersected around a single film, and how a calm and direct encounter would be at least curious, rang him. Unfortunately the given telephone numbers had been discontinued.
8 The Venezuelan bourgeoisie conceive of themselves as separate and different from other Latin American countries. Lucia Astier, a Venezuelan filmmaker living abroad, explains that 'they have a "European mentality". They like to see things from outside. You can't think in that place, it's so full of hatred' (interview with author, August 2005).
9 The BBC's reputation from an earlier imperial epoch still carries through. To take a recent example, during the second Gulf War many Americans who dissented from the views of their government found the BBC's coverage more congenial than US networks and felt that its reporting was relatively objective.
10 The term Roland Barthes appropriates from Aristotle to denote common sense, right reason, the norm, general opinion. See 1977a: 165.
11 The petition was created by El Gusano de Luz (the Worm of Light) and written by Wolfgang Schalk; see http://www.petitiononline.com/gusano03, page 7 (accessed 11 December 2004).
12 Ibid.
13 1–9, 10–109, 6010–6109, 11510–11609.
14 Propaganda is a term often deployed with the purely pejorative meaning of intentional falsehood; in fact, a more accurate definition would be the concerted action

for the spread of opinions and principles.

15 Although the final C in the acronym BBC literally stands for 'corporation', ironically it is the centrepiece of a non-profit-making public service institution that is non-commercial in both structure and function.

16 This level of Internet access should be seen in proportion to the 6,463,600 cell phone users (2002 figures); see *The World Factbook*, available at: http://www.cia. gov/cia/publications/factbook/geos/ve.html (accessed 6 August 2005).

17 Interview with author, 30 June 2005.

18 As the French philosopher Michel Foucault reminded us: 'Freud and Marx – they still have much harm to do one another.'

19 *Vertigo* is an independent film magazine that I initiated with Channel 4 funding after the demise of *Independent Video*; Marc Karlin was its first editor.

20 Ironically, Gunson is thanked in the acknowledgements in Richard Gott's book *In the Shadow of the Liberator* and Gott explains: 'He is an old friend who became disillusioned after Nicaragua, got into some bother in Cuba and took a very strong turn against Chávez. He kindly put me up when I was writing some of the book, but I think he was faintly embarrassed to be associated with it when it came out.'

21 Richard Gott, email to author, 25 November 2005.

22 Mark Woods, email to Brendan McCarthy, 7 January 2004.

CRITIQUE

1 The filmmakers assembled an extensive Dossier as a formal response to the complaints – a combination of explanation, argument and photocopied documentation: Book 3, Document J, 462.

2 The Condensed Version summarises the arguments in the Dossier.

3 Dossier, Book 3, Document K, 464; also Condensed Version Section K, point 31.

4 The filmmakers' dossier, dated 24 January 2004, comprises three separate versions: 'Summary Version of Response to Allegations' (five pages); 'Condensed Version of our Response to the Complaints' (44 pages); 'Comprehensive Version of our Response to the Complaints' (three books: Book One: 1–124; Book Two: 125–304; Book Three: 305–498). This quote here is from Summary point 29.

5 Summary point 29; Condensed Version, points 31, 32.

6 Dossier, Book 3, Document K, 465.

7 Summary point 21.

8 'Politicisation and Polarisation of Venezuelan Civil Society: Facing Democracy with two Faces', paper delivered at the 14th International Congress of the Latin Ameri-

can Studies Association, Dallas, Texas, March 2003, 8–9.

9   Maria Pilar Garcia-Guadilla writes: 'a group of retired military, many of whom had business links with security firms, allied themselves with the representatives of middle-class neighbourhood associations and designed the "Community Plan for Active Defence" which was to be applied in private residences.' She suggests that there was a particular build up of this activity in anticipation of 23 January 2003, the date on which the birth of Venuezuelan democracy is celebrated because of the fall of Marcos Perez Jimenez in 1958 (2003:19).

10 Transmitted by BBC2 in October 2003.

11 Summary point 22.

12 OFCOM Provisional Adjudication on the complaint of Mrs Fiorella Morales, 28 September 2005.

13 OFCOM Provisional Adjudication on the complaint of Ms Adriana Vigilanza, 28 September 2005.

14 Photographs taken by Maurice Lemoine and his account of the incident are published in *Le Monde Diplomatique*, July 2002. Compare this with Gregory Wilpert's personal eyewitness account (see Wilpert 2007b).

15 Summary point 6.

16 Special Broadcasting Service. TX October 2002; transcript reproduced in Dossier, Book 1, Document B, 75–81 and Book 2, Document D, 200–03.

17 There were 19 fatalities that day: seven had participated in a pro-Chávez demonstration, seven were anti-Chávez and five were non-partisan bystanders. 69 were wounded: 38 in a pro-Chávez march, 17 in the opposition demonstation and 14 were reporters or unaffiliated bystanders.

18 *Forever Mozart* (France/Switzerland, 1996).

19 Summary point 2.

20 Summary point 8.

21 Lucia Astier is a pseudonym. She requested the use of this name because she felt that to become overtly involved in the argument would jeopardise her access to the contending parties in Venezuela.

22 Email to author, 29 January 2004.

23 See http://www.globovision.com; also reproduced in Dossier, Book 2, Document D, 229–36.

24 Summary point 14.

25 Summary point 18.

26 BBC News website: Venezuela Country Profile (http://www.news.bbc.co.uk; accessed 6 August 2005). The CIA website indicates that 47% remain below the poverty line (1998 estimate) according to *The World Factbook* (accessed 6 August

2005).

27 The filmmakers give the date of the article in their Dossier as 10 December 2002.

28 The filmmakers give the date of the article in their Dossier as 16 April 2002.

29 Condensed Version, 22.

30 Dossier, Book 3, Document L, 480.

31 Venezuela Solidarity UK (http://www.venezuelasolidarity.org.uk; accessed 20 June 2004).

32 Or Dang Nhat Minh, Vietnamese feature director, quoting Anton Chekhov: 'L'art – c'est le detail, et plus le detail.'

33 *The Devil's Excrement*, available at: http://www.blogs.salon.com/0001330/2005/08/17.html. (accessed 7 August 2005).

34 Letter from David Best, Programme Executive, OFCOM Programme Standards & Fairness, to Diane Goldrei, BBC Programme Complaints Unit, 28 September 2005.

REFLECTIONS

1 Conversation with author in Galway, 27 September 2002. This proposition is outlined in detail in Eaton (1997: 40–3).

2 An echo of some sense of this in the sequences of the Leader arriving by plane through the clouds/mist is deployed to very different political ends in Leni Riefenstahl's *Triumph des Willens* (*Triumph of the Will*, 1935).

3 It can be further argued that film itself as a form cannot equal the succinct and complex analytical power of written discourse; film's significatory practice possesses elements (image, music) offering pleasures which lie elsewhere. These do not approach the precision and exact ambiguity of the word.

4 General Jorge García Carneiro describes a pivotal meeting of military commanders at the Ayala Battalion at 1p.m. on 12 April in Guevara (2005: 133–6).

5 Lucia Astier, email to author, 29 January 2004.

6 The filmmakers told the author that when they enquired, the tape of this programme was 'missing from the television station's archive'.

7 John Grierson's foundational phrase defined documentary in a balanced and open way. Interestingly his own work with Len Lye, Norman McLaren and others embraced a wider range of expressive and even non-figurative forms.

8 Rephrased from Renov (1993: 31).

9 Interview with Malcolm LeGrice, 10 October 2004.

10 Given as between three and six months' output.

11 The terminology and ideology of 'balance' has been directly challenged by the Glasgow University Media Group in *Bad News* (1976), *More Bad News* (1980) and *Really Bad News* (1982).

12 This programme encountered a storm of criticism from sections of the press and, like *The Revolution Will Not Be Televised*, an investigation took place after the event; the inquiry's findings largely cleared the programme of any impropriety, although it noted a number of errors.

13 I was caught up in this controversy as *Mother Ireland* (Derry Film and Video Workshop, 1988) contained interview footage of Mairéad Farrell, one of the three IRA operatives. A short account of the banning of this programme can be found in the *Oxford Encyclopedia of Censorship*. For broader issues of the media in relation to the Northern Irish conflict see Curtis (1984) and *Ireland: the Silent Voices* (Rod Stoneman, 1983), transmitted by Channel 4 on 7 March 1983.

14 Andres Izarra became director of Telesur, the new pan-Latin American satellite channel, and is currently Minister of Popular Power for Communications and Information.

15 All shares in Guardian Media Group are owned by the Scott Trust, at the time of writing chaired by Liz Forgan, whose remit is to safeguard commercial success while upholding 'honesty, cleanness [integrity], courage and fairness'.

16 Alex Bellos, email to author, 30 August 2005.

17 Eric Hobsbawn, telephone conversation with Richard Gott, April 2002, reported to author.

18 Interview with Richard Gott, 30 June 2005.

19 Fuelled by a disaffected BBC journalist like Robin Aitken (see 2007).

20 Research into media reporting in the Vietnam War indicates that most Americans perceived the media as hostile to the war, although this is not borne out by a statistical examination of actual reporting.

21 Shock troops used by Pinochet's regime to terrorise and coerce. An article with the front page headline 'The Venezuelan *cara pintada* has arrived' was published in the Buenos Aires newspaper *El Clarín* while Chávez was in prison and was taken up in Uruguay and Paraguay (see Guevara (2005: 84).

22 Richard Gott suggests 80% (see 2001: 172). However, Greg Wilpert puts 'realistic figures' for poverty when Chávez came into office at around 65%; email to author, 20 June 2007.

23 'I was working there in the late 1980s and remember them flying their children to Miami for school everyday', was an impression repeated by a Moroccan filmmaker at a screening of the documentary in Marrakech, 6 December 2006.

24 Significantly Chávez had a 70–80% approval rating in the first year he was in office;

Greg Wilpert, email to author, 20 June 2007.

25 A significant effect on the outcome of the campaign was to get everyone, especially immigrants from other Latin American countries, to register to vote.

26 In 1998 the votes were as follows Chávez: 3.6 million/56.25%; opposition: 2.8 million/43.75%. In 2006: Chávez: 7.3 million/63.48%; opposition: 4.2 million/36.52%.

27 'He is going to make Venezuela a launching pad for communist infiltration and Muslim extremism all over the continent … We have the ability to take him out, and I think the time has come to exercise that ability.' *The 700 Club*, broadcast on the Christian Broadcast Network, 22 August 2005.

COMMITMENT

1 Email to author, 29 January 2004.

2 Interview with Franco Solinas (1927–82) conducted by PierNico Solinas (no relation to the writer) in 1972. It was published with the original scenario for *The Battle of Algiers* and was republished in a booklet that accompanied the Criterion Collection DVD release in 2004.

3 The effect of their dialectical point of view may be gauged from the fact that a VHS cassette of this film was being circulated by active Republicans in the Falls Road, Belfast, in 1984, when I met Richard McCauley, Sinn Féin's Press Officer; and it was also screened for senior government operatives in the Pentagon's Special Operations and Low-Intensity Conflict office in August 2003 at the beginning of the second Gulf War.

4 Apparently in Germany after 1933, Gestapo interrogators were able to spot Marxists and KPD (German Communist Party) members by the use of the word 'concrete' in their discourse during interrogation.

5 Press conference hosted by Ken Livingstone at City Hall, London, 15 May 2006.

AFTERWORD

1 The previous chapters of this book were written before February 2006; the material in this chapter was completed in late 2007.

2 Gregory Wilpert's meticulous and balanced exposition of the provenance and potential of twenty-first century socialism in *Changing Venezuela by Taking Power* (2007) also assesses the points of weakness and criticism.

3 Francis Fukuyama's *The End of History and the Last Man* (1992) expands on his 1989 essay 'The End of History'.

4 See also Tarasov and Zubenko (1984).

5 16 April 2002, reproduced in Golinger (2006: 182–7).

6 Statement issued by Simon Wiesenthal Center on 4 January 2006.

7 *L'Offensive médiatique contre le Venezuela continue, Le menonge de l'antisémitisme* (Caracas: Ministry of Communication and Information, 13–14).

8 In remarks to the Associated Press on 5 January 2006, Rabbi Arthur Waskow offered further historical precision – 'It was the Roman empire, and Roman soldiers who crucified Jesus.'

9 Insight into the mindset of CIA operatives is provided by the extensive email exchanges between retired senior CIA covert operations officer Rudy Enders and Andrea Zimmerman between December 2004 and March 2005 as part of the latter's unpublished PhD thesis *Secreting History: the Spectral and Spectacular Performance of Political Violence* (Central Saint Martins College of Art, University of the Arts, London, 2007).

10 Interestingly Telesur managers announced their intention to form a cooperation agreement with Al Jazeera whereby the station, based in Doha, Qatar, would open a central office in Caracas. According to Izarra the deal was never concluded. See Kozloff (2006: 127; fn 83).

11 Conversation with author, 30 June 2007.

12 Conversation with author, 1 October 2007.

13 'Photography, in the hands of the bourgeoisie is a terrible weapon against truth' (Brecht 1998).

14 Conversation with author, 30 August 2007.

15 Email to author, 17 October 2007.

16 *Constitution of the Bolivarian Republic of Venezuela* (Caracas: Ministry of Communication and Information, 2006: 10).

17 Translated quotation from an anonymous paper published under the Ávila TV, Media Analysis Workshop, July 2007.

18 The Independent Media Center and local versions such as Indymedia Ireland are media collectives, with independent volunteer journalists creating 'radical, accurate and passionate tellings of the truth'.

19 Seóna Ní Bhriain, who had previously worked with the media collective Paper Tiger TV in New York, wrote an illuminating account of her experiences in Caracas: *War of the Worlds: Reality/TV in Caracas* (unpublished).

20 'Venezuela: Democracy and Social Progress', City Hall, London, 28 October 2006.

21 A vision emanating from *Lost Horizon*, a 1933 novel by British author James Hilton; the harmonious valley's provenance in the imperial imagination is indicated by its mysticism, exoticism and isolation from the outside world.

22 Antonio Gramsci, historic leader of the PCI and Marxist theorist, elaborated a ver-

sion of historical change that allowed for a greater degree of cultural and national difference. As Chávez put it in his PSUV foundational speech: 'We are going to relaunch indigenous Venezuelan socialism inspired by our own roots' (2007: 47).

23 In the months before he died, Philip Agee sent a draft speech that he intended to deliver at the Huston School of Film & Digital Media, Galway, as part of a European Solidarity Tour, 'The Five Cuban Prisoners – Defending Against Terrorism', email to author, 17 October 2007.

24 Speech at luncheon hosted by Ken Livingstone at City Hall, London, 15 May 2006.

FILMOGRAPHY

Anatomy of a Coup (SBS, TX: October 2002).

Enter the Oil Workers (Bolivarian Circle of the Global Women's Strike, Venezuela, 2004).

¿Puedo Hablar? (May I Speak?) (Christopher Moore, USA, 2007).

Puente Llaguno: Claves de una masacre (Llaguno Bridge: Clues of a Massacre) (Ángel Palacios, Venezuela, 2004).

Say the Truth! (Ministry for Popular Power for Communication and Information, Venezuela, 2007).

Talking of Power (Global Women's Strike, Venezuela, 2005).

Venezuela a land with many missions (YORVIDA Productions, Venezuela, 2006).

Venezuela – A twenty-first Century Revolution (Global Women's Strike, Venezuela, 2003).

Venezuela Bolivariana: People and Struggle of the Fourth World War (Marcelo Andrade, Venezuela, 2005).

Radiografia de una mentira (X-Ray of a Lie) (El Gusano de Luz, Venezuela), available at: http://video.google.com/videoplay?docid=-3378761249364089950.

BIBLIOGRAPHY

Agee, Philip (1975) *Inside the Company: CIA Diary*. Harmondsworth: Penguin.

Aitken, Robin (2007) *Can We Trust the BBC?* London: Continuum Press.

Ali, Tariq (2006) *Pirates of the Caribbean: Axis of Hope*. London: Verso.

Amis, Martin (2002) *Koba the Dread*. London: Jonathan Cape.

Anon. (2002) 'Venezuelan President Resigns After Coup', *Guardian*, 12 April, available at: http://www.guardian.co.uk (accessed 28 June 2005).

Armengaud, Jean-Hébert (2006) 'Le credo antisémite de Hugo Chávez', *Libération*, 9 January, available at: http://www.liberation.fr (accessed 6 August 2007).

Barnouw, Erik (1993) *Documentary*. Oxford: Oxford University Press.

Barthes, Roland (1972) 'The Structuralist Activity', in *The Structuralists From Marx to Lévi-Strauss*, ed. Richard and Fernande DeGrange. New York: Anchor, 148–54.

_____ (1973) *Mythologies*. St Albans: Paladin.

_____ (1977a) *Image – Music – Text*. Glasgow: Fontana.

_____ (1977b [1972]) *Writing Degree Zero*, trans. Annette Lavers and Colin Smith. New York: Hill and Wang.

Bellos, Alex (2002) 'Ousted Chávez Detained by Army', *Guardian*, 13 April, available at: http://www.guardian.co.uk (accessed 28 June 2005).

Benjamin, Walter (1973) 'Theses on the Philosophy of History, VI', *Illuminations*. London: Fontana, 255–66.

Brecht, Bertholt (1998 [1955]) *War Primer*, ed. and trans. John Willett. London: Libris.

Burns, John (2003) 'Irish film on coup "twisted the facts"', *Sunday Times* (Irish Edition), 30 May, 7.

Campbell, Duncan (2003) 'Chávez film puts staff at risk, says Amnesty', *Guardian*, 22 November, available at: http://www.guardian.co.uk (accessed 4 August 2008).

Campbell, Joseph (1993) *The Hero with a Thousand Faces*. London: Fontana.

Chávez, Hugo (2007) 'Speech of Unity', *Socialism of the XXI Century Publications*, 1, January, 17–51.

Corner, John (1996) *The Art of Record*. Manchester: Manchester University Press.

Coronil, Fernando (1997) *The Magical State*. Chicago: University of Chicago Press.

Curtis, Liz (1984) *Ireland: The Propaganda War*. London: Pluto Press.

Debray, Régis (2007) 'Socialism: a Life-Cycle', *New Left Review*, 46, July/August, 5–28.

Delacour, Justin (2004) 'Anti-Chávez Pollsters Panic', *Counterpunch*, 7 August, available at: http://www.counterpunch.org (accessed 20 June 2005).

Dinges, John (2005) 'Soul Search', *Columbia Journalism Review*, July/August, available at: http://www.cjr.org (accessed 26 November 2005).

Eaton, Michael (1997) *Chinatown*. London: British Film Insititute.

Eisner, Hanns and Theodor Adorno (1994 [1947]) *Composing for the Films*. London: The Athlone Press.

Ellis, Jack C. and Betsy A. McLane (2005) *A New History of Documentary Film*. New York: Continuum.

Ellner, Steve (2007) 'The Trial (and Errors) of Hugo Chávez', 28 August, available at: http://www.venezuelanalysis.com (accessed 2 October 2007).

Ellner, Steve and Daniel Hellinger (2003) *Venezuelan Politics in the Chávez Era: Class, Polarization, and Conflict*. Boulder, Colorado: Rienner.

Ellsworth, Brian (2007) 'Venezuela replaces anti-Chávez TV station with state network', *Irish Times*, 29 May, available at: http://www.irishtimes.com (accessed 6 August 2007).

Enzensberger, Hans Magnus (1976a) 'Constituents of a Theory of the Media', in *Raids and Reconstructions*. London: Pluto Press, 20–53.

_____ (1976b) 'Tourists of the Revolution', in *Raids and Reconstructions*. London: Pluto Press, 224–52.

Fukuyama, Francis (1992) *The End of History and the Last Man*. London: Penguin.

_____ (2006) 'History's Against Him', *Washington Post*, 6 August, available at: http://www.washingtonpost.com (accessed 28 September 2007).

Garratt, Chris and Rod Stoneman (1982) 'Filmmusic', *Arnolfini Review*, January, 1.

Glasgow University Media Group (1976) *Bad News*. London: Routledge & Kegan Paul.

_____ (1980) *More Bad News*. London: Routledge & Kegan Paul.

_____ (1982) *Really Bad News*. London: Writers and Readers.

Godard, Jean-Luc and Jean-Pierre Gorin (1970) 'What is to be Done?', *Afterimage*, 1, April.

Golinger, Eva (2006) *The Chávez Code: Cracking US Intervention in Venezuela*. Massachusetts: Interlink.

_____ (2007) 'A Revolution is Just Below the Surface', 28 September, available at: http://www.venezuelanalysis.com (accessed 2 October 2007).

Gonzales, Juan (2005) 'Chávez Surprise for Bush', *New York Daily News*, 19 September, available at http://www.zmag.org (accessed 24 October 2005).

Gott, Richard (2000) *In the Shadow of the Liberator*. London: Verso.

_____ (2005a) 'Chávez leads the way', *Guardian*, 30 May, available at: http://www.guardian.co.uk (accessed 28 June 2005).

_____ (2005b) 'Giving the Finger to the US', *Guardian*, 26 August, available at: http://www.guardian.co.uk (accessed 23 September 2005).

_____ (2005c) *Hugo Chávez and the Bolivarian Revolution*. London: Verso.

_____ (2007) 'The battle over the media is about race as well as class', *Guardian*, 7 June, available at: http://www.guardian.co.uk (accessed 7 June 2007).

Goumbri, Olivia B. (2007) 'Is the Price Too High for Beneficial Public Broadcasting in Venezuela?', 27 June, available at: http://www.venezuelanalysis.com (accessed 6 August 2007).

Greene, Graham (1984) *Getting to Know the General*. London: Bodley Head.

Guevara, Aleida (2005) *Chávez, Venezuela and the New Latin America*. Melbourne: Ocean Press.

Guillermoprieto, Alma (2005a) 'Don't Cry for Me, Venezuela', *New York Review of Books*, 52, 15, 6 October, available at: http://www.nybooks.com (accessed 5 October 2005).

_____ (2005b) 'The Gambler', *New York Review of Books*, 52, 16, 20 October, 24–6, 34.

Gunson, Phil (2002) 'Reporters on the Job: Mean Streets', *Christian Science Monitor*, 16 April, available at: http://www.csmonitor.com (accessed 7 August 2008).

_____ (2004a) 'Documentary: Director's Cut', *Columbia Journalism Review*, May/June, available at: http://www.cjr.org (accessed 20 May 2005).

_____ (2004b) 'Chávez: Inside the Con? Documentary and the Fabrication of the "Truth"', *Vertigo*, 2, 7, Autumn/Winter, 30–1.

_____ (2005) 'Inciting self-censorship', *Economist*, 12 March.

Harnecker, Marta (2005) *Understanding the Venezuelan Revolution*. New York: Monthly Review Press.

Hilton, James (1933) *Lost Horizon*. Project Gutenberg Australia: http://www.losthorizon.org.

Jones, Bart (2008) *¡Hugo!* London: Bodley Head.

Klein, Naomi (2003) 'The Media against Democracy', *Guardian*, 18 February, available at: http://www.guardian.co.uk (accessed 28 June 2005).

Kozloff, Nikolas (2006) *Hugo Chávez: Oil, Politics and the Challenge to the US*. New York: Palgrave Macmillan.

Lambert, Stephen (1982) *Channel Four Television with a Difference*. British Film Institute.

London, Kurt (1970 [1936]) *Film Music*. New York: Arno Press.

Luttwak, Edward (1968) *Coup D'État*. Middlesex: Penguin Books.

Macdonald, Kevin and Mark Cousins (1996) *Imagining Reality*. London: Faber.

Mackenzie, Suzie (2003) 'Out of the Ivory Tower: Interview with Jacqueline Rose', *Guardian*, 4 January, available at: http://www.guardian.co.uk (accessed 5 August 2008).

MacShane, Denis (2002) 'I saw the calm, rational Chávez turn into a ranting, populist demagogue', *Times*, 13 April, available at: http://www.timesonline.co.uk (accessed 8 August 2007).

McArthur, Colin (1982) 'Raid on Entebbe: Constructions and Repressions', in *Dialectic*. London: Key Texts, 121–5.

McCaughan, Michael (2002) 'Filmmaker describes the overthrow and return of Chávez', *Irish Times*, 16 April.

_____ (2003) 'Seeing is not believing', *Irish Times Weekend Review*, 26 July, 6.

_____ (2004) *The Battle of Venezuela*. London: Latin America Bureau.

McKee, Robert (1999) *Story*. London: Methuen.

Mair, Peter (2006) 'Ruling the Void?', *New Left Review*, 42, November/December, 25–51.

Márquez, Gabriel García (2000) 'The Enigma of the Two Chávezes, Deliberate Ambiguity Breeding Doubts and Hopes', *Le Monde Diplomatique*, 4 October, available at: http://www.zmag.org (accessed 11 December 2004).

Marx, Karl (1845) 'Part 1: Feuerbach: Opposition of the Materialist and Idealist Outlook', in *The German Ideology*, available at: http://www.marxists.org (accessed 7 September 2008).

Massari, Roberto (2005) *Hugo Chávez tra Bolivar e Porto Alegro*. Bolsena: Massari editore.

Nichols, Bill (2001) *Introduction to Documentary*. Bloomington: Indiana University Press.

Orwell, George (1949) *1984*. Middlesex: Penguin.

O'Shaughnessy, Hugh (2005a) 'Chávez still popular as opposition remains divided', *Irish Times*, 15 September.

_____ (2005b) 'Hugo Chávez – Showing the US Who's Master', *New Statesman*, 10 October, available at: http://www.newstatesman.com (accessed 11 October 2005).

_____ (2007) 'An Irishman's Diary', *Irish Times*, 8 May.

Palast, Greg (2003) 'Hugo Chávez is Crazy!', in *Abuse your Illusions*, ed. Russ Kick. New York: Disinformation Press, 10–17.

Perelman, Marc (2006) 'Venezuela's Jews Defend Leftist President in Flap Over Remarks', *Forward*, 13 January; available at: http://www.venezuelanalysis.com (accessed 14 February 2006).

Raby, Diana (2006) *Democracy and Revolution: Latin America and Socialism Today*. London: Pluto Press.

Renov, Michael (1993) 'Towards a Poetics of Documentary', in Michael Renov (ed.) *Theorizing Documentary*. New York: Routledge, 12–36.

Rockett, Kevin (2003) *Ten Years After: The Irish Film Board 1993–2003*. Galway: Irish Film Board.

Sánchez, Alex (2007) 'Mercosur, CAN and the EU: how will Venezuela manage foreign trade?', available at: http://www.spectrezine.org (accessed 6 August 2007).

Staff and Agencies (2002) 'Venezuelan President Resigns After Coup', *Guardian*, 12 April, available at: http://www.guardian.co.uk (accessed 28 June 2005).

Stoneman, Rod (1992) Sins of Commission', *Screen*, 33, 2, Summer, 127–44.

_____ (2001) 'Recycled Electrons: Film and the Digital', *Kinema*, Fall, available at: http://www.kinema.uwaterloo.ca/stonm012.htm (accessed 14 September 2005).

_____ (2005) 'Sins of Commission II', *Screen*, 46, 2, Summer, 247–64.

Suárez, Roldan Tomasz (2002) 'Venezuelan Coup, Five Facts about April 11th', *Counterpunch*, 12 June, available at: http://www.counterpunch.org/suarez0612.html (accessed 20 June 2005).

Sussex, Elizabeth (1969) *Lindsay Anderson*. London: Studio Vista.

Tarasov, Konstantin and Vyacheslav Zubenko (1984) *The CIA in Latin America*. Moscow: Progress Publishers.

Vogler, Christopher (1998) *The Writer's Journey*. Studio City: Michael Wiese.

Ward, Paul (2005) *Documentary: The Margins of Reality*. London: Wallflower Press.

White, Michael (2002) 'Egg on face of Labour Minister who called deposed leader "ranting demagogue"', *Guardian*, 15 April, available at: http://www.guardian.co.uk (accessed 12 December 2007).

Wilpert, Gregory (2007a) 'RCTV and Freedom of Speech in Venezuela', 3 June, available at: http://www.venezuelanalysis.com (accessed 3 June 2007).

_____ (2007b) 'The 47-Hour Coup that Changed Everything', 17 June, available at: http://www.venezuelanalysis.com (accessed 17 June 2007).

_____ (2007c) *Changing Venezuela by Taking Power*. London: Verso.

Winston, Brian (2000) *Lies, Damn Lies and Documentaries*. London: British Film Institute.

Wright, Amaranta (2005) *Ripped and Torn*. London: Ebury Press.